NO OTHER CITY

Published by Ethos Books

Ethos Books is an imprint of Pagesetters Services Pte Ltd

Blk 2, Pasir Panjang Road,
#07-09/10, Alexandra Distripark
Singapore 118481.

Published with assistance from Publishers Grant Scheme

NATIONAL ARTS COUNCIL

ISBN 981-04-2276-8

Front and back cover photo by Alvin Pang.

Photos on pages 33 & 95 by Ian Lim. On page 143, background photo
by David Tan, insert photo by Zaheer Baber.

Design and produced by Pagesetters Services Pte Ltd.
Printed in Singapore.

NO OTHER CITY

THE ETHOS ANTHOLOGY OF URBAN POETRY

Edited by Alvin Pang and Aaron Lee.
Foreword by Professor Dennis Haskell and
Afterword by Tay Kheng Soon.

TEXT CREDITS

In order of appearance. Copyrights are held by the respective poets unless otherwise stated. All poems are reproduced with permission.

SECTION I

SECTION III

ACKNOWLEDGEMENTS

The Editors would like to thank

Professor Dennis Haskell for his foreword and insightful introduction (thus saving us the embarrassment of trying to write an academically credible analysis of the book ourselves).

Mr. Tay Kheng Soon, whose vision, passion and ardent advocacy of a truly 'cultural' Singapore inspires us to do our own little bit.

All the writers in this anthology who gave us their wholehearted support and much encouragement and advice. This book belongs to them most of all.

Special thanks to the indefatigable Ms. Ho Poh Fun for her timely advice, and whose peerless networking put us in touch with several of the writers who were otherwise not accessible.

The inimitable David Tan who generously put his fabulous photography at our disposal. Thanks also to Ian Lim, Pascal Pong, Terence Heng, Professor Zaheer Baber, Reuben Soh and Gerard Koh for contributing their wonderful images to this project. Also, Nelson Tan for hooking us up with the right grapevine.

Lei Ying, for (what else?) patience, patience, patience, late nights and patience. Cyrus and Damienne, for vetting the poems by sitting on them with indisputable feline conviction.

Tan Gek Lin and the entire Pagesetters Team who worked tirelessly to translate our vision into the book you hold in your hands.

Mr Fong Hoe Fang for his faith beyond the call of duty. We owe you big time.

And most of all, Winnifred Wong — the Editors' Editor — who shared our vision and made sure we did something about it. Her resourcefulness, enthusiasm, deadlines and hip little pad are the reason why this book exists. We can now sleep at night.

No spouses, cats or dogs were harmed (we hope) in the production of this book.

CONTENTS

SECTION II

FOREWORD

In his verse autobiography, *The Prelude*, written at the time that Raffles came to Southeast Asia, Wordsworth recalled the most astonishing thing about living in late-18th century London: a place of "streets without end" (l.133), "all specimens of Man/ .../and every character of form and face" (ll.236–38):

> ... Above all, one thought
> Baffled my understanding, how men lived
> Even next-door neighbours, as we say, yet still
> Strangers, and knowing not each other's names.
> (ll.117–20)

The Prelude provides the first detailed account in English of the city as we have known it in the 20th century, and many in our own time have been led to a similar spiritual bewilderment. Coleridge in "Frost at Midnight", lamented having been "reared/ In the great city, pent 'mid cloisters dim". The answer of the great Romantics was to retreat to the country, finding in nature profound spiritual sustenance. Remembering daffodils "dancing in the breeze" sustained Wordsworth in the city, as they flashed upon his "inward eye".

Two hundred years later, Singapore poets might feel that they experience this situation in infinite intensity, with no daffodils in the mind to help. In a talk given at the National University of

Singapore in December 1999, Philip Jeyaretnam pointed out that
the Singapore writer's situation is claustrophobic; in a city-state
there is no escape from the city, there is no country to go to.

The status of the city is, of course, more complicated than I
have alluded to so far, for complexity is of its essence. Even
Wordsworth was fascinated by its "every character of form and
face" (I.238). The city is the place of anonymity and alienation
but also of variety and interest. These contrasts between the
city and country have often been elaborated, in all cultures. In
Chinese culture the city within the city was the "Forbidden
City", a place the ordinary person dare not enter — the site of
grandeur, power and danger. The contrasts are illustrated in
works as diverse as Shakespeare's *Henry IV* (both parts) and the
fable of the Town Mouse and the Country Mouse. The city is
the site of sophistication, artifice, danger, interest and compli-
cations; the country is where the bumpkins live, but it is the
site of sincerity. The country is safe, but may be boring — it is
the locale of simplicity. The most important experimentalist in
20th century poetry, T. S. Eliot, reacted against the poetic forms
of the Romantics but not against their view of the city — it
was the place of sophistication but of aridity, a waste land.
More academically, and by contrast with Eliot, Anne Brewster in
writing a study of Arthur Yap and Philip Jeyaretnam, argues for
the city as "a zone of indeterminacy where two or more cultural
referential codes cohabit, and where identities are consequently
'in the making' or 'in process'". This is a view of the city as
possibility, its artifice allowing for the conscious construction of
identity. Identity is chosen, not given, and is never fixed.

These ideas appear in various guises in *No Other City*, the first poetry anthology to pay attention to Singapore as a *city*-state. This is a Singapore seen in relation to age, class, fashion, gender, history, popular culture, literature and race — a nation small enough to have some of the intensity of a neutron star socially and politically, but with that strong sense of a wider world and other possibilities that education and reading bring. The range of attitudes expressed is commensurate with the number of poets included, from the established to the new, and together the poetry provides a fascinating portrayal of Singapore at the turn of the new millennium.

Professor Dennis Haskell
University of Western Australia
Perth, February 2000.

INTRODUCTION

I.

Sometime in 1999 we invited, via the press, word of mouth and the Internet, anyone and everyone to submit poems for a new 'anthology of urban poetry' to be published in 2000. We left it to those interested in submitting poems to define 'urban poetry' for themselves. We ourselves had, at that time, only some vague notion of what kind of poetry we wanted to see.

In the ensuing weeks, we received several hundred poems (primarily and significantly through e-mail), most of which were submitted by writers, young and not-so-young, who were not part of the known literary circle in Singapore. This was our first pleasant surprise. The next was the encouraging discovery that many of these poems, though written by poets unknown to us, were of a high quality. Many of the writers were students or professionals in fields ostensibly far from poetry. Surely, this represented a groundswell of awareness, expression and urgency, the roots of which went deeper and broader than anyone had imagined? Given that the average personal volume of poetry takes several years for even accomplished writers to put together, it was understandable why such a rich range of voices had escaped notice — there have simply been no formal channels of expression for writers who had a small body of good work, but which did not have the guidance, experience, portfolio of work, or opportunity to get themselves published.

But why urban poetry in particular? Since we started AFTERwords as a public literary discussion forum in a downtown bookstore in late 1997, it was apparent to us that there was an increasing number of young people writing poetry in English. They read and talked about poetry with a passion and urgency that suggested that it was more than merely a way to pass time, or to express themselves. It was a handle on life, a way to grapple with the issues of growing up in a city that was changing before their eyes, and far too quickly.

The pioneering poetry of our early writers had been tied to the events and spirit surrounding our independence and early nationhood. By the time the present generation of our poets was writing, however, the ultramodern city-state as we now know it had already taken hold. We had moved, in the space of a generation, from kampong to metropolis, from kopi to capuccino, from semi-literacy to palmtop microcomputers. Our writing, we realised, was and had always been trying to deal with this flux. We thought this was worth exploring more fully, especially since we were about to step over the threshold of one millennium into the next. A thematic anthology focusing on the urban experience of Singapore seemed a democratic, appropriate and timely means to look at Singaporean poetry in English as a total body of work.

We decided early on that the urban poetry anthology should include a diversity of voices and levels of experience. We would include published works alongside the new material at hand; this would anchor the new work with the foundation laid by existing poems in print. This meant that these unpublished works would have an immediate context, a tradition to which they could contribute. At the same time, this book would bring together the work of both established and new writers in a manner which would accentuate their common thematic concerns. The poems have thus been sequenced, not by poet, as many anthologies are wont to do, but by their thematic relevance to the poems coming before and after them. We wanted to generate the strands of a kind of seminal dialogue between poems, leading to a discernible tapestry across the entire anthology. Thus, Boey Kim Cheng's "The Planners" is set next to Edwin Thumboo's "The Way Ahead"; Leong Liew Geok's "Trees Are Only Temporary" is seconded by Joshua Yap's "remembering trees". Eerie resonances emerge between the works of poets who at first glance have little to do with each other in terms of age, experience or poetic concerns. We believed that this would lead us most truly towards a mapping, however tentative, of our common urban and human landscape as expressed in our poetry.

So we selected poems without preconceived design, but for resonance and relevance, as well as for the strength of the writing. We consciously side-stepped the more obvious cases of angst with otherwise (we felt) little literary merit, and with some regret left out pieces which we thought showed promise but were not fully formed enough to warrant inclusion. We were out to look for new voices and perspectives of the city. Two main principles then governed our selection of works from published writers. First, we would as far as possible look out for new or recent poems from them. We are delighted to be able to include new poems from writers such as Alfian Sa'at, Toh Hsien Min, Daren Shiau and others, as well as from more mature writers like Kirpal Singh and Angeline Yap. We were also able, due to the fortuitous release of their new volumes, to include some of the new work of Leong Liew Geok, Heng Siok Tian and others who had been recently published. Our second principle was to avoid, where possible, poems which were canonical or had been much anthologised. We wanted to revisit the work of established writers, focusing on relevance rather than reputation or political correctness. Where a poem was well-known, we would include it only if it served as an invaluable thematic anchor for the pieces around it, or if it highlighted a prevailing trend of thought. A case in point is Robert Yeo's much anthologised "Christian Cemetery", which neatly rounds up many of the recurrent themes present in the first section of the anthology.

The idea for the three sections which structure this anthology came later, after an eventful editorial retreat, and much further reflection and meditation. Suffice to say we were hunting what we were not sure even existed — an organising principle for the anthology, which would bring together all the underlying motifs, skeletal patterns and driving forces present in this diverse body of work (only ostensibly about the city, urban living and the urban landscape) while doing justice to the unique resonances and concerns of each individual poem. We grouped the poems by broad thematic clusters, further paring down and refining our awareness of the emergent patterns. The end result surprised us most of all.

What emerged from the cacophony of voices and visions was a continuum of thematic issues into which most, if not all, the poems fell. More significantly, this thematic trend also reflected to a rough extent the broad chronology of the poems involved — older works, or poems from the most established writers thus tended to fall within the early half of the spectrum, while newer voices and pieces gravitated towards the opposite pole. We had apparently stumbled upon an evolutionary trail of recent Singapore poetry and its developing themes, with some hints of where the trend might take us. It is not our purpose to analyse to any scholarly extent the implications of such a poetic continuum — it is rather our intent to present it as best as it has revealed itself to us. The division of the anthology into three sections marks shifts in focus, and are arbitrary mile-stones in the continuum, rather than hard boundaries. We have done so more to assist the interested reader, than to confound the passing academic.

Aaron Lee and Alvin Pang
Singapore, January 2000

II.

The postmodern view of the city as a place in which identity is chosen and always in flux emerges partly out of the pace of city life, and partly out of its obviously made quality. The most fundamental difference between the city and the country is that the city is constructed by humans, whereas nature is constructed by God or other forces outside the human, a given to which humans must adapt themselves. This constructed characteristic of the city is especially apparent in Singapore, which is the postmodern city par excellence. It may be steamy near the border with Johor Bahru but in Singapore proper, people move from their air-conditioned cars to air-con workplaces, air-con shops and air-con homes. Singapore is a place where you can go to a few different climatic landscapes on a manufactured Night Safari, and see (cardboard or plaster) snow down Orchard Road at Christmas. Singapore is a city of endless possibilities but of an accompanying sense of inauthenticity. Here, all the features of the city enunciated above are featured, except perhaps danger— although dangers of special kinds exist. Multi-ethnicity, and government attitudes that make it almost impossible to separate one's self from one's role as citizen, further complicate individual identity here. Cities are sites of potential freedom partly because the anonymity that life within them allows for an acceptance of difference, but difference and freedom are somewhat curtailed in Singapore. The degree of experiment allowed is constrained, culturally and politically, although traditional ethnic cultural differences are permitted and, in fact, abound.

Multiple ethnicity, wealth, education and a thriving tourist industry all make Singapore a city of great cultural interaction. Singapore can rightfully advertise itself as a place where east meets west, providing a cultural richness, special possibilities in the use of English and other languages, but also uncertainties which the writers in this anthology can be seen to be working through. It is still possible to be Romantic, even in the year 2000, but it would be impossible to be a Romantic in Singapore. None of the poets here writes with anything like the values of Wordsworth or Coleridge. This is the result of cultural imperatives, not physical ones. Philip Jeyaretnam was right to stress that Singaporean writers have no countryside to retreat to, but they have wealth, education and an international airport. Singaporeans can find the whole world open to them, at least on a temporary basis; few of the writers have not travelled and that experience of other landscapes and cultures is one which informs their sense of identity when back in Singapore. Add to this the technological awareness of Singaporeans (which is second to none in the world) and the existence of the Internet, and it becomes clear that Singaporeans' sense of themselves and of their society must be seen in a global context. Implicit, unannounced comparisons are everywhere apparent in the poems of this anthology.

Gwee Li Sui addresses Singapore as "City of/Endless Energies" ("Kenosis"), a two-edged quality since it means the endless building and rebuilding on the same sites which is often mentioned in *No Other City*. This rebuilding means a possible loss of cultural memory, as Felix Cheong declares "till the crumbling past/is no more than a concrete heap" ("Work in Progress"). Boey Kim Cheng notes that "history is new again" and that "the drilling goes right through/the fossils of last century" ("The Planners"). Even the Singapore River is so changed that as Lee Tzu Pheng observes, "you can hardly tell/her history" ("Singapore River"). This worry about Singapore perpetually destroying its own history, and consequently creating a shallowness of identity in the present, is further developed in Lee's "Amoy Street Houses". Seeking history and cultural meaning in daily lives, the poet tries to look at a Chinese face looking at her. That face is "pressed against the window bars" of an Amoy Street house "in the shadow of the giant/bank tower" but also against the window of time itself. In the poem's conclusion, it is not clear whether the face is looking "out on us" from the present or from the past.

A troubled sense of Singaporeans' relationship (or non-relationship) to nature appears in many poems. To Tan Bee Kee the city-building cranes constitute a "bitter parody of Nature's grace" ("Cranes") while Leong Liew Geok's "Trees Are Only Temporary" mocks the official sloganeering of Singapore as "garden city", since it is discarding nature for a "fever of estates and shopping centres" as fast as possible. For David Leo, what is lost in this process is "dignity" ("Trees"), since nature is a world that we share with other creatures, whereas estates and shops comprise a world that is solely human. Ho Poh Fun exclaims, "amazing how the present has the past/so neatly encapsulated in silence" ("katong"), and many of the poets express concern about a world in which humans are completely in control. Paradoxically, this creates a feeling that the individual is less in control than ever. When the city-state is officially portrayed as "doing/feats of a lion in the body of a fish", to quote Gui Wei Hsin in "A Prophecy Disclaimed", the poets feel that something is awry.

Inevitably, there are thematic overlaps in the three sections of this anthology. In the second section, on life in the present, Caleb Yong expresses concern about "a blind rush for progress and prosperity" and, in a nicely ironic phrase, "the religion of pragmatism" ("Turning to Exile"). He is also worried that the city sets up the terms of people's lives and that, robotically, they must follow. This is a feeling shared by Dennis Yeo, whose "Urbanesque" reveals a "claustrophobic" city of "artificial ambience", where every scene is reduced to "shades and polygons". Heng Siok Tian cleverly employs an impersonal voice to portray Singapore by lists so that it becomes a city of "et cetera" ("Naming of Parts of a CDB, Shenton Way 1992"). History is then preserved only in the names of streets, which does at least give language some role to play.

If all this sounds hopelessly negative, it is well to remember Edwin Thumboo's insistence early in the book that "the City is what we make it" ("The Way Ahead"), and that individual perceptions of the same site can vary enormously. Teng Qian Xi's "Happiness" is a celebration of sensory delight, particularly in eating, which seems appropriate to Singapore. In "Neon Reflections" Charmaine Chan celebrates Singapore's "all day-glo dazzle and ultra-violet glamour" and the "bright neon stain" of its "gorgeous vari-coloured tapestry" even while trying to forget a relationship that was located there. By contrast, Dominic Soon perceives similar sights in terms of the city as "a dusty tangerine concrete grove" and returns this section to a perception of the people as robotic. He is bothered by the lack of purpose of urban life, its endless momentariness "like thoughts, here and then gone in a flash" emphasising transience, even in the apparent solidity of the city.

In the third section of the anthology, Ng Yi-Sheng provides a sharply different tone to feelings of anonymity. "Losing It" is a clever poem, playful but serious, as "I" loses "me" somewhere in the supermarket of urban life. A similar wit is evident in Angeline Yap's "Try Again Later" in which an overly machine-oriented society creates in the individual a sense of Catch-22 uselessness. Machines also loom large in Teng Qian Xi's "Rapunzel Waiting", in which romance is only possible by email. In the unfairy tale world of "optic cables", communication is only possible at one remove. This is a preoccupation in many poems here, including Alfian Sa'at's "3am on IRC" and Elaine Pang's "In Conversation". The overall effect is of separation in togetherness — the alienation experience of the city — also apparent, for Keith Tan, on the MRT ("On an MRT Train").

However, underlying some of the poems is a perception of the possibilities made available by the city's plurality. Alfian Sa'at's "Autobiography" maintains a sense of unbridled hope, while Keith Tan's "Journeys" ends in a vision of "Builders of bridges/ Defying measure". Through telling the story of his grandmother he is able to gain a grasp of history and thereby see a future "beyond the edge of any map". This is a vision of organicism entirely at odds with the more disillusioned presentation of Singaporean ambition and industriousness portrayed by Caleb Yong in "Turning to Exile".

Similar contrasts can be perceived in Luo Qining's "Sidewalk Punk" and Terence Heng's "Irony". Qining's poem is a jazz-rap performance piece which sees life in Orchard Road as performance, and rather enjoys it. "Irony" is a wonderfully wry poem which amounts to a refusal of global capitalism — a view shared by Umej Bhatia in "The @ Generation". Tangentially related to these poems is Alfian Sa'at's "What They Talk About in the Bedroom When the Children are Fast Asleep", a depiction of city alienation and self-concern that Wordsworth would have recognised immediately. This poem might usefully be compared to Arthur Yap's famous portrayal of HBD mothers' conversations, a process which could be undertaken with many of the poems in this anthology in building up a sense of Singaporean literary tradition.

The attitudes expressed in "What They Talk About" do not apply only to Singapore, a reminder that Singapore society and poetry also have an international context. The poems quoted comprise just a small part of the overall richness to be found in *No Other City* overall, and their range of tone and technique, plus the sheer contrariety of attitudes expresssed, testify to the city as a place of plurality and fascination.

Professor Dennis Haskell
University of Western Australia
Perth, February 2000.

References

William Wordsworth, *The Prelude, or Growth of a Poet's Mind* (Text of 1805), ed. Ernest de Selincourt, revised by Helen Darbishire. London: Oxford University Press, 1960. All references are to Book Seventh: "Residence in London".

Anne Brewster, *Literary Formations: Post-colonialism, Nationalism, Globalism*. Melbourne: Melbourne University Press, 1995, p.103.

I

"City of New,
bring forth sentinels who sing praises
for the demolition of what we
were"

KENOSIS

When I lose you
for my fallen love,
O City of
Endless Energies,
your eyes burn out
along the streets

and there are cries
between morning crows
(as there sometimes are)
but I have become
your mimicry,
a burnt moth's wing,

and in your lag
I will walk amid
my midnght voices
and turn a single
inner echo
to deathlessness

for this is the truth
that I hear, I hear,
as long as my passages
of beauty are framed
above sharp edges
without and within

and so, you City
of my white bread,
Demon for frail loves,

walk my broad roads
of desiring
but keep in mind

how we must trust
each other after
I have paid your bills
and tapped your lines
and know well now
why you got lost,

why you mess me up,
renounce your poor,
dim your evenings
with recklessness
and scourge yourself with
electricity

for this is the truth
that you say, you say,
as long as your passages
of beauty are framed
above sharp edges
without and within.

A PROPHECY DISCLAIMED

standing like sentinels of a dream
the skyline's towering spires extend
heavenward, where our aspirations
flare with the blue and gold of morning
we, the people, bear testament to
a prophecy disclaimed: "there was a time
when people said Singapore won't make it
but we did" and we did indeed, doing
feats of a lion in the body of a fish
strength in credit cards, leather bags
and steel buildings, cement statues;
erecting glass monuments with glowing number glyphs
reclaiming promises from the sea
which brought us here when trees still ruled the land
that now stand like dreamy sentinels
of a lush and cooler time, before
the fever came and set the island
ablaze with sound and fury

THE PLANNERS

They plan. They build. All spaces are gridded,
filled with permutations of possibilities.
The buildings are in alignment with the roads
which meet at desired points
linked by bridges all hang
in the grace of mathematics.
They build and will not stop.
Even the sea draws back
and the skies surrender.

They erase the flaws,
the blemishes of the past, knock off
useless blocks with dental dexterity.
All gaps are plugged
with gleaming gold.
The country wears perfect rows
of shining teeth.
Anaesthesia, amnesia, hypnosis.
They have the means.
They have it all so it will not hurt,
so history is new again.
The piling will not stop.
The drilling goes right through
the fossils of last century.

But my heart would not bleed
poetry. Not a single drop
to stain the blueprint
of our past's tomorrow.

THE WAY AHEAD

We were to speak, to chat,
Involve our several minds on how
To frame a City.
We were asked, judiciously, to talk of beauty
In a town, how the town would change,
Turn supply, rugged, yet acceptable.

There were the four of us,
A Professor, much travelled and artistic,
A Senior Civil Servant who knew the way ahead,
The Town Planner and I; I?
The average man, the man-in-the-street,
Feeling nervous, struggling to free
Practicalities from dreams,
Leaving a small remainder hopefully sensible.

The Professor favoured China-town, not surprisingly.
His thinking was crowded, bred by city living.
The teeming interchange of word and gesture,
The odour of ordinary lives,
Intimacies overdone or underdone,
Privacy come to grief, private grief made public,
Were seen as energies of a proper order,
As breaking the loneliness of man.
It had the right perspective, he said,
In the middle of tourist China-town.
The flats were fine, but parcelled out too neatly.

The Town Planner took a different view.
Intricacies of change were based on principles;
A flat in the sun was to be had by everyone,
A spaciousness, part of the better deal,
Politics, economics, the re-deployment of custom,
Clan and tribe. Impulses of a national kind

Gave common rights. There has been talk of heritage.
There should be change, a reaching for the sky,
Brightening the City's eye, clearing the patches
From the shoulders of her hills,
For regiments of flats.

What could I say? Or think?

A city is the people's heart,
Beautiful, ugly, depending on the way it beats.
A City smiles the way its people smile.
When you spit, that is the city too.
A City is for people, for living.
For walking between shadows of tall buildings
That leave some room, for living,
And though we rush to work, appointments,
To many other ends, there must be time to pause,
Loosen the grip of each working day,
To make amends, to hear the inner self
And keep our spirits solvent.
A City should be the reception we give ourselves,
What we prepare for our posterity.

The City is what we make it,
You and I. We are the City.
For better or for worse.

THE CIVIL SERVANT

When surgery's a necessity, who hesitates?
When it's an option, well,
that takes some thinking, doesn't it?
So it was with the river.
We lived with it for years, you see,
its notorious whiff of decay,
the bankside scum and lighter congestion,
the quaint unloading of the boats
a nostalgic reminder of a way of trade
backwatered by containers and computerization.
When the PM said, "In ten years time
let us have fishing in the Singapore River.
It can be done," well — it had to be.
But how? A labour of Hercules lay before us.
A river is a system fed by many streams;
clean the rivers meant clean most of the island.
A major operation.
When we began The Clean Rivers Campaign
we felt as if the surgeon had cut open the belly
to find the cancer spread through the body.
It involved so many — from environment,
health, sewage, drainage, housing,
pollution control, primary production —
you can imagine the problems of co-ordination.
And the result?
Farewell Bugis Street, goodbye Chinatown.

Relocate the bumboats to Pasir Panjang.
Resettle hawkers, close down the pig farms,
rehouse squatters far from their communities.
These were the costs we couldn't count.
Luckily, the river's a marvellous patient:
stop the infection and it heals itself.
"After the rains, fresh blood flows in old veins."
Now the city's heart pours its cleaner, greener waters
through a body working ever harder,
transformed in the '90's into — well,
a human, leisure-friendly river environment,
yet incomplete.
The river's renewal made the body whole
but in the process we misplaced its soul.
We can't devise an action plan for that,
unfortunately.

PHASES

Perhaps it is a phase
I'm going through —
this need to scrape out words
trapped inside untidy nails,
like scraping out accumulated oil-stains
from sides of well-used oven.

This need
to scrape words onto a sheet
like the calm sea
reclaimed for resettlement,
so the mind
dredged for techno-try.

The shoreline of simplicity
is now a postcard of scenic imagination.

Words like simplicity
have been wall-papered to decorate block offices,
tiled in with floor mosaics,
shuttled up and down on busy elevators,
left homeless on high antennae.

Just the other day
passing by dusty Shenton way,
I saw
Words unintentionally uncovered
as workers dug
for MRT tunnels.

These MRT tunnels:
undoubtedly
a phase to be going through.

CHANGE ALLEY

Alley of change utterly changed.
The name of the place names
the lost decades, the places and times
gone with our belongings, migrated
along the routes buried or closed
to the country of changelessness.

Many dark tunnels ago, a child rode
on his father's back through the trades of tongues,
the bazaar of puzzling scents and smells,
an underwater world of sailors
stale from the sea and travellers
drowned in dreams of home,

floating through its length skeined
with striplights and bare bulbs, the stalls
spilling over with imitation wares
for the unwary, watches, bags, gadgets and tapes;
in each recess he heard the conspiracies
of currencies, the marriage of foreign tongues
holding a key to worlds opening on worlds
for the wakening senses of the child.

But most it was the laughing boxes
secreting peals of ghostly glee
derisive and disembodied, which held
the mind, kept the child listening
and fathoming still through the years
as if the future was then foretold
before the alley's enchantment broke
in the dazzle of a weekend afternoon.

Later the grown man in loneliness
would return as evening snuffed out
the life of trade and the Sikh nightwatch
hauled from its silent depths a worn string bed.
Standing at its mouth he cast his stones
of questions to plumb the depths, to fetch
the echoes of consequence and distance
off all the alleys he had wandered.

It seemed he had come through the changes
unchanged, searching still the place
for signs leading home, or out of the streets
emptying into loss, whichever turn he took.
And while he waited the country flipped
the book of changes; streets lost their names,
the river forgot its source, soaring towers
policed the skies and before the answer
could come like the laugh heard changes ago

the alley packed its stalls and followed
the route to exile, its nomadic spirit
inhabiting now the country of the mind.
All is utterly changed, the map useless
for navigation in the lost city. Only an echo
remains, the man haunting and sniffing
where the alley had been, measuring its
absence till the spirit of place returns,
till a door yields at the end and he walks
out free, changed beyond all changes.

WORK IN PROGRESS

Why this upheaval
constant as our coastlines
eaten by tides,

the way streets and lands
are chewed and spat
between the pages of directories

till the crumbling past
is no more than a concrete heap
ready for another retro-fit?

We are a country of dust
where nothing is saved
but face.

SINGAPORE RIVER

The operation was massive;
designed to give new life
to the old lady.
We have cleaned out
her arteries, removed
detritus and silt,
created a by-pass
for the old blood.
Now you can hardly tell
her history.

We have become
so health-conscious
the heart
can sometimes be troublesome.

RECLAMATION

restlessly we cut
into the soil of our past,
wet with sweat of brow,
the blade of remorse
clanging against the rock of time
to unearth,
then to pack
scoop after scoop
into the wave-washed shelf
the mud of penitence
for sins long buried

how much more can we extend
the borders of our troubled turf?
how much longer stall
the incessant, relentless
beat of the ocean's roar?

BLUE-PRINT

on the destruction of West Coast Park

Suddenly, you realize those words
could not be printed on sea-water,
and what you thought were waves
beyond the palms and barbecue pits
are cunning hoardings, sea-blue running
the length of beach you used to know.
Seeing through it all you find
the shore gone, abnormally far out,
and trucks criss-crossing
where boats used to bask.
Engines erupt as giant cranes bow down,
bend to their tasks, filling up the bay.
The coast waits in tense disarray, witness
to invasion, man's power, a kind of rape.

Panicked, the birds have fled.
Heron, sandpiper, even land-birds leave
an eerie desolation; their sanctuaries,
violated, now are empty. As are the playgrounds
and the paths, deserted; not a soul
where children once chased games,
and kites pulled fliers ragged in the wind.
Nothing so forlorn as a forsaken park,
a place for people rendered inhospitable.

Warehouses and wharfs are on the cards.
The Port Authority raises its winning hand.
Nature rescinds prerogative, the sea withdraws.
Crab, clam, the boatmen and their shacks
defer to relocation, reassign their living,
subsist upon the pickings left behind. In time,
their isolation from each other will be sealed.

ROAD-WORKS

i.
Sometimes it is hard
to believe that creatures of flesh and bone
may tear up the roads like paper,
peeling the rind of the earth
as carelessly as eating an orange.
When they fall to the ground and devour it,
the scenario is one
of blasted sand, harsh talk
and machinery.

ii.
I pass, and workmen rise
from the earth as rusty as the tools
with which they cut the soil, as if
they too had resurrected from the long sleep
of rivers deep underground.

I taste the dry dust of their loud conversation,
unknown syllables flapping in my face
like strung-out laundry,
familiar and incomprehensible.

iii.
And so they make the crooked straight again,
filling valleys and levelling what mountains
there are in this country.
As I walk my fingers trace
the tape which closes them in
their subterranean habitat, constructed
miraculously with new-cut seamless lines
that join and stretch down the taut tarmac
as far as I can see,
tighter even than the coarse grip
with which they hang on
to the smooth shaft and cold steel of their reality.
Neither they nor I will ever let go.

iv.
When they pack up and leave
two months or a year from now,
they will leave behind a criss-cross
of surgical scars and giant patchwork
squares of grey and darker grey.
Almost no other sign where they had touched the earth;
no sign that is, except for that great ribboned chunk
of congealed stone and bitumen, gift-wrapped
and given back to itself.
The ground may breathe again,
though the soft-talking trees deny it everyday.

FOREIGN WORKER CUTTING TREES

In this country, the branches of tall trees
in public places are not permitted
to grow as they please

but must be regularly trimmed on
hot restless sun-drenched days
by foreign workers

carrying electric saws, who climb
with bare hands and feet up
into unfamiliar treetop territory.

Today I held my breath as I watched
one of these men make his way
twenty metres up above ground —

if he fell he would surely break a limb
or back or otherwise kill himself on
this hot, forgettable afternoon,

a thousand miles from home.
Realising this, perhaps, he kept pausing,
looking for right places to put his foot;

taking each small step with an infinite,
enduring patience. Finally reaching a safe perch,
from which he knew he could not fall.

He put down his saw in the fork of two
small branches. Wiped the sweat from
his face with the back of his hand.

And sat down, legs dangling, to rest a while,
and catch the view from a treetop.
It struck me then, how simple

how harsh, life could be. You thought only
about one thing at a time. Where
to step next. How to cut a branch. How not

to fall. How not to think of your wife or lover,
back bent, planting padi seedlings in
the rain-soaked fields

of another country. While your days
slipped by, up in the leafy treetops
of a foreign land. You could think,

as long as you liked, on these hot
endless afternoons. There would always
be enough trees for that.

NATION-BUILDING

The steady *klunk, klunk, klunk*:
construction resonates across still air
from across the street where I live
where workers hammer
stone, wood and metal assiduously
building houses they can never
dream of, much less live in.
The heavy silence of a hot afternoon
breaks, and the dust slowly rises.
I wonder about these nameless people
about their families, their wives,
sons and daughters back home
waiting…
for the money to lift them out of poverty
for the wailing babies to be fed
still waiting
for their father to return
Do they know
the hardships
occasional hostility
abominable squalor
pernicious masters
or how that money he slaves for
is a pittance here, among the rising
office towers, sleek continental restaurants,
Gucci scarves, Chanel 5 in the air.
All so very post-colonial.
He is little more than a beast
of the modern burden
building…building…building
the dreams of a nation
bound, if nothing else,
by apathy.

MADE OF GOLD

*"The villagers were told that if they put their hands on the walls of
Tekka market, money will flow out."*
— The Straits Times, August 23, 1998

This too, is an image of ourselves:

Walls that bleed money.
Dusty streets lined with gold.
Wave after wave, a babel sea
of dreamers on our shores. They build
our towers like cliffs, strong
against the sky. They build our homes
and our temples. In return
we lead them to our gods. Some are blessed.
Others learn to stretch a day's pay
for weeks, to be looked oddly upon
without flinching, to eat
with cracked hands.

> *First they take all my money.*
> *Then they take me to JB in lorry*
> *later go to Singapore in tour bus.*
> *I hide in luggage hole with five others.*
> *I scared. They just push us in like that*
> *Now I know they crooks but too late.*

> *I cannot go back they will kill me I owe so much.*
> *I cannot pay back enough. Agent take my passport*
> *then dump me on the streets of Tekka. I wash*
> *dustbin I scrub dump I sleep sometimes I eat.*

> *This all I got after working a*
> *year. If only someone told*
> *me the walls of Tekka*
> *are not made of gold.*

INDIA, LITTLE BY LITTLE

No one exists for even an instant
Without performing action;
However unwilling, every being is forced
to act by the qualities of nature.
~ Bhagavad-Gita

moon over serangoon, tide upon endless tide
of men flood the long road and alleys
like the indomitable Ganges
overflowing from the Rochor Canal

dressed in Sunday best, they teem and gather
retying knots of friendship
away from their *dharma*, their daily duty
talking, walking, letting pain
numb until suffering and joy are equal
until courage, until immortality

standing in the open spaces, in hundreds, they are the soldiers
on the battlefield of Kurukshetra
passing time while Arjuna, their nominee of despair
fights his conscience

they know now that pressing palms
on the walls of Thekka will not bring gold:
all the gold is with the jewelers
so they cut to and fro like aimless buffaloes
raising the blare of conches from the road,
watch pale *rajas* with their wives and fat children
spend riches in the shops,
maul at their desire along Desker
or just babble, babble, Babel,
building towers with their conversations
like the citadels they build by day

by sunrise, they hide their hopes in hard hats
coaxing each hour that it may earn,
gathering new bricks for their dream return

GOING HOME FROM CHURCH ON BUS 197

Going home from church on bus 197
I thought how quickly new thoughts of heaven
Transubstantiate into old residue.
I looked around. There were only a few

Fellow travellers, eyes free of vision,
Heavy heads lolled in humble submission
To heat and dust. The mind recognises
In an instant, immune to surprises,

Its failure to connect dust to sleeping dust.
I thought, people are still people, and rust
Still rust, steel still steel; there is nothing new.
The bus rattled its metal cage and a queue

Of Thai workers stumbled, with careless eyes,
To the back seats. One, of the largest size,
Jabbed the window with insistent finger
And rapid mouth, sharp verbal reminder

Of their difference. The youngest replied,
His smile in his voice. A third supplied
A joke; all laughed, even the quiet one
In the corner. Touched with the light that runs

Across the ridges of their faces, I say:
Why do these men, living between narrow days,
Catch the sun of a passing moment and
Make me feel the alien in my own land?

SUBURBAN ESTATE

*"some deserved more and got less,
some deserved nothing, but why confess?"*

crab claw walk —
don't expect a better allusion
to the lost beaches,
the only illusion
being an overcooked reddish crab claw
flung on the heathen asphalt
from some bloated beer BBQ
party.

spitting your tongue, sour,
at these low-rise leering houses,
discreet
and all,

you could see it's obvious
the suburban kids' bikes
have gotten bigger
with their fathers' Beemers;
and someone along the lane just
acquired a second Merz.

there is no victory for these,
you think,
the final justice for those
who'd appreciate better divisions
than social class,
and you —
you who sneer at the smell
of Bangladeshis sweating in the aircon bus.

THE FLAT-OWNER

You did not make this place,
had no hand in poising these
sixteen stories against the air.
You only live here and, living,
alter its space.

To a shallow cement floor,
the colour of dust and shadow,
which once was perhaps sky,
you brought the colours of wallpaper,
stereo and TV sounds, a bed,
a fridge, stove and pans and
the kitchen sink,
and potted plants to green the living room.
And this is sufficient
                    (you always think it is enough).

Now, a storm mounts at night, out of
the quiet and the dark,
rattling your windows
until the familiar view is lost in the downpour.
Now you cannot sleep,
cannot settle on an unrattled dream
but are continually waking.

Later in the storm-washed morning,
drained of all colour,
a mynah will settle on the sill and
call and call
then wing away.

You will turn in your bed
thinking of family of friends of
voices in the flat,
of this flat and its potted garden
in the wet day's early light,
and know the untamed symbol of air
had come, northern and beating,
to remind its tenant
where his breezy dreams lie.

PROVIDENCE

"... she's mortal
But by immortal Providence, she is mine"
Ferdinand
~The Tempest, Act V Scene I

propping our kampong huts on stilts,
raised over mangroves and lallangs;
      our houses aspired

now, our houses stand
on all floors

stacks, in columns, towers
across the island
propping sky and soul

these are not prophecies
      they are promises.

BIGGER, NEWER, BETTER

You must notice me — this close by the road —
Renewed, enlarged, I am spacious:
My built-in area has moved
Into attics, spiral staircase, new rooms
With blue-tinted French windows.
Marble walls and granite floors
Gleam like polished glass.

Balustrades and balconies frame
Kingly dimensions. I sit,
Facing south, on good *feng shui*,
Looking down on houses across;
Those on either side, I've nudged
Into proper place. Higher than the tallest
Tree in the neighbourhood,
Wider than the largest house,
I am one of a kind.

The chandeliers are Austrian
The glass bricks imported
The furniture is French
The drapes and fittings custom-made
The marble Italian
The carpets Indian
The vases Chinese

Like a fortress, I'm wired
Against strangers and invaders —
My alarm screams loudest and longest;
Day and night, the air-conditioning
Hums to keep everything, everyone
Cool and well-preserved.
Two maids keep up with me
Continually; lucky master,
Lucky mistress; lucky children!

My porch has room for three
Cars all parked in a row:
Red Bee Em for luck,
Green Rover for use,
Gold Merc for show.

Without plants to cut and trim,
The gardener watches ten new palms,
Cleans the swimming pool and patio gouged
Out of the garden, walks the dogs
And keeps *koi* happy and fat.

Passersby gawk at my girth.
Trying to recall my predecessor,
Their stares climb colonnade to roof;
They gulp, amazed that so little land
Could turn into an edifice.

TRAIN RIDE

out of a country drugged with
its modernity and its self-image

we rumble into
plantations and
expansive fields
where cows and
goats mull over
long grasses

we stop at
restful towns
with quaint names
where scrawny
kids scratch and
point at commuters

perhaps we have been too long in
pigeon holes, our claustrophobic comforts

how were we to
know that our
smiles could wear thin,
our eyes tire of green,
our minds hunger
for throbbing crowds,
concrete dreams?

THE JOYS OF CONCRETE

When I consider the magnificence of concrete, I am astounded. Concrete makes mounds, makes moles, makes mountains out of molehills. Lascivious men who live in concrete holes, who carry large lumps of anger in their hearts, hide in cubbyholes of concrete. Lashing at their secretaries, they vie for the affections of their telephone operators and typists. Concrete drips all around them.

Footsteps click on concrete, ticking away like the clinking of gold teeth on hard pretzels. The ceiling seep downwards their tears of asbestos, spotted with suppurations of fungal foetidness. Muzak loosens its lilting foolishness all around — the sounds of bells, trumpets, violins, the marinations of tunes we once loved — a choral group raises its proclamations in hosannas of vulgarity. Hallelujah to concrete!

Gravel, dirt, packed like almighty sand castles, waiting for the tides of time to wash them away. Dummies dressed in crimson colors, preening in the sheen of gleaming mirrors. Marionettes posing for the ultimate consumer's passion, for the glandular manifestations of abdicated princes and bag people.

Here I am in concrete heaven. Concrete under me, concrete above me. Three white towels, three face cloths, three hand towels. Hot air, cold air, sliding windows — tempting to glide away from concrete. Do Not Disturb when I repose in concrete.

I have a concrete cream: Woman with shimmering hair, body like a mango, feet planted in earth, arms full of leaves and flowers, clover in her pubic hair, serenading the morning and the horizon. Five armored creatures drag her away to a concrete bath, encase her in concrete, pour concrete in her ears, in her mouth, in her nose, in every orifice. Confess! Confess! You are a prisoner of concrete, you are the mistress of concrete, you are beloved of concrete, you are a concrete princess. See this limber limb — see how it stiffens in concrete. See how the skin puckers up and dries in the mummification of concrete. Darling of concrete! Daredevil of concrete! Concretize me! she shrieks. Cake my face, cake my toes, cake my crack!

O carnalized concrete, concretized carnival, deliver me from the inundations! Cast me into the warm waves of the crashing Caribbean, so I can meet the other casualties of concrete. Castigate all who speak against concrete. Let the professors and customer relations managers of concrete clamber into new heights of concrete. Concrete, concrete! Make poetry of concrete, make marvellous paeans to the imponderable coolness of concrete!

URBAN JUNGLE

These grim gray blocks like fingers
stretched unto the heavens,
casting shadows meters long.
Like grand trees that grow together,
filling the skies with their branches and leaves.

We like ants puny beneath,
scurrying about at your feet.
And when you fall, we run in fear,
digging up pieces we hold so dear.

These leaves we hold and raise up high,
make me constantly question why
we need to see the sky before we breathe;
why we are so bound by man-made laws
that we sigh without cause, without pause?

ANIMAL FARM

We live in a chicken coop:
just enough holes to see the light,
just enough room to make us stay
within prison walls — no real windows —
all too high up, all too small.

Through one I see a portion
branch, twigs, leaves and pretty all,
and I believe it belongs to a large tree,
craggy with age, each groove telling a story.
How it stretches to spread its arms, trapping
wind which breaks off the brittle veins. As they
fall gently to moist soil, the branches
wave to the eyes inside this
chicken coop. The wires strangle

though they don't even touch our
numb and thickened skins. We can
hardly breathe. Punishment on our
backsides — they ache upon the
chocolate coloured chairs that never change,
even with time. The rusty legs with
missing rubber hoofs: a dying horse
with a wounded leg, breathing its last....

Who screams? Not the tables, not
the chairs, not even living things
surrounding inanimate objects.
Intangible souls of tangible bodies —
they pray for the coop to crumble.

IN PURSUIT OF PERMANENCE

Tilted is good.

A serrated skyline, that seems higher each year than the one before.
Slashing in futility at the unreachable sky.

Not too much, maybe half a right angle.

People move fast, in concentric circles…
Living their short tragically tantric lives.

Looking up,
We don't have to see them.

There is green,
Large patches of green hereabouts and thereabouts…
With ochre and blotches of black in between.
Like camouflage paint on an infantryman.

Transient ourselves
We choose to chase the sky.

The angle widens
Serration climbs

But we'll tilt our necks
till they break to be free.

FREEDOM

A few suggestions:

It is the building of islands of sandcastled sanity out of the tide of the
ocean too small to live on but dry enough for a moment to breathe;
It is composing your own constellations from a given square of a given sky
and forgetting their names in the morning when you count the sun;
It is dancing without steps or remarkable shoes to the sound of everyday,
keeping your place in a queue of citizens waiting for a necessary item;
It is cagesong —
It is a flying machine
that obeys the laws of physics.

And daring to mention
what flowers you want at your funeral.

PARADE

we have come to bid farewell
to a wise and wonderful officer
who has led us to greater heights
inspiring us from that swivel chair of his
while the men spat with vengeance
the bitter mingle of sweat and rain

we have assembled now
like neat stacks of green dominoes
on a decorated parade square
(that is not even square)
cradling our weapons
waiting to hoist them
in a salute that must surely
scrape the sky

the eddies of heat seethe
from the face of tar
eating into my boots
(gleaming stupidly with kiwi)
swirling around
the curl of my fists

LEADERSHIP IS WHAT I CAN GET FROM YOU (BASTARDS, DON'T YOU EVER KISS ASS?)

Our camp commander — this was only so because he had shown great integrity, leadership skills and all roundedness to the instructors — was yelling at us: it was the first day of camp, his face was a big o and his mouth was a big o, o people, he shouted, you guys have not woken up yet, so all of you — do twenty pushups now, he made it seem so easy, and I wanted to yell at him: I can do that too, stand there and tell others to do fucking pushups, and the rest of us without these leadership qualities went down o onesir, o twosir, o threesir, like countless waves breaking upon the sandy shore.

ARMY CAMP, PARADE GROUND

Tortured ground. Your skin is blistered
by the vehement boots that stamp and stomp
all day long. The unconcerned sun applies
itself to both human and asphalt alike
And when the rain comes, your heaving sighs
are vapour mists that rise out from your pores.
Relief in little steaming clouds of past parades.

Torture ground. You are the place where the
teardrops of our fatigue fall and evaporate.
The slamming of rifle butts and rubber soles
massage your unrefined features. Leaves and
twigs are gingerly swept away every morning
so as to leave you, and us, presentable.

CENOTAPH

Like a lighthouse or misrendered spire
Rising forty feet from shooting cars,
In this thawed time when nations aim far higher,
It stands, to mark the dead of two world wars.

OUR
GLORIOUS
DEAD

Is chiselled in the hard granite obverse.
Five steps, a step for each year's bloody wounds,
Bear tourists up. Their inconspicuous
Black digits disappear in traffic sounds,

As ancient letters on the wing are worn
Into a craggy mask. In rest above,
Again for man's use never, steeled from scorn
And various disgraces, names which served:

Achurch, Adcock, three times Anderson,
"They died that we might live" behind,
With "Nicholas loves May" sprayed at the end,
And fulgid green leaves to the steps consigned,

While one withered weed titubates on the peak
Atop a lion knocker. The wreathéd crown
Is suitably implacable, the bleak
Black knobs in rank defend the sombre stone.

Few stop in passing by. A humble myth
In time, each day amassing abandonments:
The only people round this monolith
Are young skateboarders practising their stunts.

AT THE FUNERAL PARLORS, SINGAPORE CASKET COMPANY

"Perhaps the past is a paper house"
~ *Patricia Ikeda*

Pastor John in platform shoes walks to the boom
box on the concrete floor, bends down and turns
the knob till the volume hisses, "WE SHALL
MEET BY THAT BEAUTIFUL SHORE." Red-hot
ginger blossoms gape among maiden-hair fern,
their musk jabbing like carrion.
A pale lemon giant worm, you lie embowered
beneath more bouquets than lovers or children
had delivered to your door. "What honor!"
someone whispers of the calling cards
from the corporate brother's rich associations.
They fall off frangipani leis, names engraved
like so many gold-rimmed kinfolk.
This moment is new. Disbelief lies
on your waxy cheek. Before the sermon
Pastor John invites a prophetic bond with me,
the daughter from New York. I have arrived
decades late, after the red Singapore-
chopped aerogrammes that urged Scripture
and held out for attention.

Then the charismatics
are gone: the Chinese pastor headed for Los Angeles,
greying ladies and lonely Tamil adolescents,
minor bureaucrats whose Christ raises the dead,
who are looking for nothing your island can offer.

I also leave you, to gawk at the Taoist shaman.
He stacks pyramids of gold paper bricks
before the Chinese funeral room next door.
I watch for his unknown dead as he
pours brandy over the extravagant wealth
and sets the conflagration with a Cricket
barbecue starter. Electric blue Mercedes
models and towering skyscrapers
flash up behind acetate Maytag deep freezers.
The black-hatted paper man in coattails
toasts crisply down to a twisted heap.
Casually the Taoist jumps over the fire, once, twice,
three times. Lifting black robes above his pants
he clears the flames. The bamboo scaffolds burn slower,
glowing after the papery ash collapses,
after you have been delivered
to the crematorium accompanying
Christian smoke and ash into the earth.

CHRISTIAN CEMETERY

These tombstones have been uprooted.
Chipped madonnas and broken crosses,
all weathered grey, are strewn on grass.
Never thought I would see them thus.
These stones that have been here so long
it seems the land was theirs for good —
but for the Urban Renewal Department
which needed that plot for a park.

My granny, though Catholic, was cremated
according to her wish. She knew
room in our affections was all
the space she needed. Or perhaps
she'd heard all about urbanization,
how her stone, had she been buried,
would wear away or be dislodged.
And so when she had to give up
what space she occupied, she left us
something that cannot be lost in stone
and therefore fears no renewal.

BLOCK 39

Strange how memories cling fast to a number.
The years spent trekking from one neighbourhood
of the old housing estate to another,
never examining the route until
the road is not travelled any more.
Brief Significance inheres in loss still;
all else is commotion in Singapore.

I am astonished by the human power
to carve a home out of a concrete block,
to decorate a space, to grow a flower
in corridor gardens, to boldly dry
underclothes on public poles in heat waves.
But equally I am astonished by
how we leave our homes like so many caves.

Is this the basketball court I grew up in?
Jumping zero point, playing tua-bei-long,
one day the police, the next the thief, catching?
Watching subtly quiet girls watching me,
looking up to that big boy, delirious
with living, admiring his healthy
brown body, to the whistle oblivious?

Was it from this room I left the City
of Destruction, carried my own burden
and struggled with myself, proud and guilty?
Was it from this woman I learned the art
of living: how to handle fork and knife
at a buffet, how to trust, how to start
a chit-chat, how to assemble a life?

Everything in me wants to say yes, settling
the claims of the past decisively, and
borrowing fresh loans to see me through, crossing
the straits on rope-bridges spun from before.

Are there straight lines in life, like in poetry?
Surprising how little I feel, as doors
are closed the last time on rooms clearly empty.

Poetry must help to remember, but can a
poem generate, like a power station,
a homesickness where there is none? Or be the
gravestone to which we make our pilgrimage,
a permanent sacred relic? Can we
build in stanzas prayer rooms for old age?
Poetry, perhaps, is then necessary.

II

"people, trees, buildings, things
draw boundaries, set
barriers, and shape
your sense of identity;

if you lie face to sky,
stare into space and far
surpass senses' reach, you
forget who and whether you are"

TURNING TO EXILE

i.
In the mists of uneasy dreams,
an unhappy nation shakes itself from bed
and squeezes into starched uniforms prepared dutifully
the night before. Tired strands of hair must be
brushed off the collars and lifeless
breakfasts swallowed like ice cubes.
A door is unbolted and a groaning bus
flagged to meet a not yet risen day.

ii.
Time now for a people to avert their eyes,
to look down and look away from the unsightly
silence of impotent cries. The day steals past,
and in a horrifying catacomb of offices,
factory worklines and stuffy classrooms,
the gospel of breeding walls is endlessly erected.
The people breathe in, and out again, believing
their decision is lazy, their dreams flushed down
a drainpipe because they have eaten the
flesh of rules. More and more they force
the life out of their bodies, as if squeezing
pus from a wound. "This is our lot,"
they intone, "we will keep our place.
"We will teach our children to sacrifice
their names for the perfection of schools,
we will teach them to take candy
only when they have thrown the others behind."
There are no exceptions, for all are made guilty.

iii.
Here in this city, three million people
are steeped in the religion of pragmatism,
dislocating the backbone of truth in favour
of a fossilised morality and Good Asian Values,
that the pride of our hands may lend applause

to deafen the pity of our wooden puppet bones,
empty of marrow or blood. Nor the piety of
bent knees nor the heady salsa of humanity
for our Moral Fibre. All three decades it has been
a blind rush for progress and prosperity.
No force can stop this locomotion into the dark.
Every man and woman and child drags along
the path of a formula life, sleepy in non-fiction
work that numbs the mind and heart.

When it all becomes clear, if ever, we will
realise the sun has set. We will look
at our children and ask why they were born
to be crammed indoors and deprived of seeing
another face until the doors re-open at dusk,
when tiredness hangs on the eyes of the parents
like a cancer. Some struggle for the satisfaction
of the performance, and others struggle because
that is all they know. Like a cancer, my people.

How we collapse under all the gravity.

iv.
Of course there are those who do not even
work. The people do not touch them,
they bear a sting only to themselves.
We know them well because we are
taught to despise them. They are the
loud mouths and long hair we have
come to accept as a phase of our young.
Their place is not considered, theirs is seen

as an age of angst, as if slippery feelings were
untrue. The people shake their heads,
pretending that they no longer yearn,
fidgety with anticipation, for some kiss.

And yet their actions betray them.
Circling in their houses and through the
street, they think they will find
life in the romanticism of late nights,
life in a huge campfire of activity,
life in becoming a social lighthouse
to world-weary bumboats, life in the
breaking of greater and still greater boundaries.

v.
Perhaps, though, the undecided may be
forgiven. Everyone knows there are those
who still linger naked with subversion —
they are the ones whose vulnerable
groins we have kicked. We stand aside
laughing as they stoop over, clutching
in pain. They have not learnt
the road to progress and it is only right
for the moral citizen to help them.
And so the people stun them with glaring eyes,
and soon, with a shaking of heads, cast
them away into a muddy wilderness
where they can no longer be found.

All this, in accordance with the mantras
of the Nation, is justified.

vi.
This is the way it has been
and this is the way it will be.
Nothing will get better and nothing
will get worse. Everything has been
clicked into the endless plans of perfection,
everything sacrificed to the god of the
Good Life. Why should the mortal be given
a place in our society?

Children will grow up to see
friends falling away into this abyss,
becoming pantomines in a theatre
of cruelty and numbness.
This will be called their
idyllic childhood and gyrating youth.
"Come to terms with this reality,"
mock the Brahmins of the State.
"This is a country where righteousness
can only be found in exile, where that biting
loneliness that carves out space for a heart
feels not like a blessing, but like gall."

Because every person that wishes to
open his mouth, and penitent and prone,
rush into the world with sharp knowledge
and a nodding of decency and difference,
can only hope to drive himself away.

Accepting neither the lightless inside
nor the numb nakedness of the
outside, he can only hope to tread
the suffocating gulf that stretches between.

SCRAPS OF A WEEK

night:
>   looking at the neighbouring block
>   red eyes glow in dark rooms
>   I move in worshipful stealth

driving instructor says:
>   don't whistle during lesson please
>   it's rude, you know

in Mandarin, coffeeshop woman:
>   hai, you only want small change is it?
>   you wait ah
>   I've gotta do my business first

sunlight:
>   young Malay girl on rollerblades
>   her ankles wrapped in silver
>   she speeds by shiningly, frock flapping

waitress to our table:
>   sorry
>   we've run outta carrot soup
>   I've brought chicken noodle soup
>   you want?

Bishan bus-stop:
Chinese housewife lets her sons
>   one after another urinate
>   *ssh-ssh* at the kerb side
>   her gold bangles make metallic music

train station, Yio Chu Kang:
    I buy a Transitlink farecard
        part of a series called Blue Paradise
    incongruously it's got a picture of
            a crown of thorns starfish

night again:
        such dreams of the unchristian creature
     spiky monsters gobbling coral
          colonising the unpeopled seas.

MAN OF '99

The man of '99 has no idea
he is being strangled by his own fine details
intricate affliction brought from yesterday's
today which really

is tomorrow's inherited sweet fury
a bitterquick aubade to welcome the ash
of the swinging sun that faces the city
of ostentation

Wasting from his time-wrought fatigue
worn under a sunken shroud of pliant black eyes,
aching back and sore heart choked with
caffeine

Bound hands looped loosely around fraying shoulders
tightly round subdued neck and feet
forcing his ornate head face to face
with the grey dirt of work,
his pale nemesis.

THE SOBERING AGE

Isn't it too early to feel jaded already
since it's before the appropriate age?
You stop frowning and for that matter
smiling, because of your fear of wrinkles.
You succumb to the infomercial's promise
of a less prosperous Middle Kingdom.
You start to salvage the lost loves you forgot
to claim at nineteen, a more glorious year.
But the women reassure you that they
did not see the premature graying of hair-roots.
As long as the wallet is fed. And for that reason,
you straighten your tie and remember work.

NAMING OF PARTS OF A CBD, SHENTON

One part is streetly directional.
CBD is Shenton Way,
road names being
Cecil, Robinson, Cross,
Maxwell, Anson, Collyer.
(Some discreetly colonial.)

One part is bloc blockbusters,
usually termed Towers,
Buildings, Centres.
There are Robinson Towers,
CPF Building, et cetera,
OUB Centre,
Shenton House, et cetera.
DBS Securities,
et cetera,
Inland Revenue Department,
et cetera,
multi-storey
proposed projects
et cetera
et cetera
et cetera

One part is landuse,
deftly defined by
"Restricted Zone" where
value-varied vehicles,
assembled valueless
as sardined-slabbed metals
during office peak hours.

WAY 1992

one part healthy haste
one part haloed history
ghosts of john little
johnston bonham
robinson and company
crumbled continuity
sepiaed stories
archival postcards
at commercial raffles square
early horsedrawn carriages
made way for popular rickshaws
obsolete tramways
poor competitors
with flavoured mrt fare
applied assessed land value
fluctuated rubberily
when it came to
change alley and sailor streets
value is subjective
timing deadly determining

One part is crisp suites,
white long sleeves,
leather stilettos,
Shenton Way girls of Battery Road.
Hub of credit,
facilities,
facsimilies,
facile credibility.
Executive rites are handphones,
credit-cards a-calling,
co-ordinated socks,
compatible stockings.
(Call it upward mobility.)

(Only very recently
a famed Victorian structure
of Lau Pa Sat
is considered picturely,
enigmatic.
There is also a needful CID
quietly amidst cosmetic concrete.)

Today,
textbook urban geography
derides:
urban crisis, dislocations, rank, dynamics,
segregation,
income re-distribution
become
shell-shock casualties of possessive politics,
isolation
daily disguised poverty.

Lines, lies, lives are lease-worthy.
The business of verse
is not landed property.
A listing is in keeping
with Shenton Way lyrics.

down the line

i.
the wind that weaves across buildings
carries the calculus the city is reckoned on.
call it what we will, it is liquid graphics,
neither statistics nor logistics can propel,
for its basis well under the skin has yet another
lined in rubrics & this, then, is palpable
& lends the eye whatever enchantment it wishes.
it will enchant with the cool young shadows
the sun, climbing vertically down windows,
leaves behind. it will enchant in its repose
by moving, shifting to the centre of its axiom,
in its layering of reality & in imparting
the sum of its being; every part, every space
larger & more real than the entirety.
if tomorrow someone sings a confessional
of some 'ism or other, the refrain sinks in
as only a totality & any event, being given,
predetermined, is at the onset already silent.
silently, the moon flanked by ribbed clouds
is jailed for influencing, or not, missiles
& this too holds no stored fear for tomorrow
it rains & the gurgling of drains, protomusic,
will soothe ancient nerves, irons out new alarms.

ii.
we say that a person who had stabbed himself
19 times & then thrown his own body over
the balcony is unbelievable reportage.
if you tell me times enough, tired, i will believe
or, at the least, agree. & if you tell me
times more, angered, i will throw
the narrated body back at you.
possible, too, i well might have believed.

so credulity is a bigger commodity than credibility
which is everybody's. the other, an exercise
of the mind, is yours if you can shape it.
breaking it, breakage is accidental
& never really necessary. a place-style
of impelling rhetorics, down the line,
foisting tautologies as ramifying definitions.

iii.
the tanned figures on the beach are not there
for further sun. noon, the heart's pulsation
without speech, is already late enough.
tenacious as weed, the crabs secrete bricks
& lay at the water's edge a library of margins.
page by page, it prefabricates the day's
ins & outs but, like pure callisthenics,
seems never quite enough. created thus to grow,
the calculus will help or quell us.
i thought the ground had foretold all.

a habit by which the world moves, people will not
look at the centre of things. the custodian must
find some flaw about his own belief to show up
those, accusing him, as punitive. wrong,
that in his pursuit, he does them good
purely by chance. such coincidence is a gift
&, in these days of libs, isn't it lib & let lib?
when the verb fails, everything ancillary
has only its chronicle of current antiquity.

grass replaces grass, fast. down the line,
dry, roots are cast. garden-to-garden green grass
calls to the eye an explication of beauty
& beauty, in the colouring heart of the beholder,
is not what suffices or does not. that it does not
comes last.

iv.
what everyone will tell you is what everyone
wants to hear, has been told. the clouds
have no radio & cannot relay silver linings,
glosses, appendices. we hear, what told,
wheels of woe, a battery of ear-assault
pooling in the lymph. the years,
if they have brought us no wisdom, would have
exploded the myth our images hold, rearranged
the calefaction of the thermometer
we regulate by.

SUNBATHING

You know nothing of the city,
our city does not permit
even a memory of the sky.

My daily life
made up my days
the same without let up.

O for a windfall of days
that are without deliberation,
without architecture.

The sun a burgeoning eye
at point blank
on me.

Let my long-untaught senses
simmer then,
excite a blunt consciousness.

OF SPITTING

Scorching white sun
                    shone
                    on a bridge
                    where,
                    bent badly
                    like a T-square,
                    a burnt oldman,
                    grappling with lean black bars,
                    cringed into a sha-
                    dow of an acute angle,
                    echoes of misshapen, yet
                    strangely familiar sounds tear-
                    ing through the griped vice of
                    his convulsing mouth,
                    frothing white around
                    his scrawled lips,
                    while
                    pencilled shades
                    flittered so fast
                    past him, that
                    even their erect shapes
                    were erased to
                    nothing

                    later,
                    below the bridge,
                    at the bus-stop,
The sky, spat, sad.

EQUATORIAL

We were born into this:
Clogged pores, clammy limbs,
Sweat which itches and stains
Collars and armpits, souring nostrils.
Wrapped in blanket sheath,
Plants aren't pierced by ice
And trees don't save for spring;
A yellower sun burns harder,
Foilage throws a greener rash;
Fruit and flower clash for brightness
And rain's soap opera, the monsoon,
Drenches us into missing the sun.

Wet or dry, we use walkways, porches,
Umbrellas, trees whose shades —
Probed by tentacles of heat —
We swelter in. Let tourists bake
Themselves on sand. We love our
Air-conditioned places, at least
Till evening draws the sun-shy
And the breeze, if there,
Takes the humid out of circulation.
Through day, by night, the nature
In which termites breed unseen
And appetites cease only for death
Takes no rest: the equatorial floods
Profligate air, saturating.

CROW

taut to a "Z",
these windows' reflections
testify to a Saturday's stillness
like grim guardians of privacy —

until it takes a sharp sliding
cut, diagonal to the HDB face,
from the winged Zorro
of a silent crow.

HAIKU BITES

i.
Singaporean monk
on a shiokedelic binge.
Makansutra, lah.

ii.
In my street Singlish
I order a hamburger.
McCity moment.

HAPPINESS

It's at times when I see sunlight
spangling through the treetops
and the world freezes in a single
dazzling instant of green and silver
or when I'm with friends beside
a fountain wolfing down scraps of
roast chicken with oil all over my fingers
and the black-pepper taste of
chicken in my mouth weaves with
the sound of everyone laughing
and the colour of water-drops falling
like ballet dancers. It's realising with a
startled pang: *there is nothing more*
to want right now. I want nothing more
than this.

URBANESQUE

i.

streets, extending past the boundary of
sky and earth, along paths of droning,
motorised noise; melding into a public
landscape, a massive claustrophobic complex
humanised by ceaseless shifting
over concrete surfaces.

edifices surround, transfixing the
cloud-buffered sky above: permanent hives
of transient activity, operating
on airconditioners and office politics,
artificial ambience and stacks of dried pulp.
along the roads hurtle myriads of cars and other
mechanical animals. sideways the city
looms, sudden, and slowly, in time-lapse photography
buildings change exteriors and attract buzzing
crowds.

ii.

row upon row of repeated flats
blot out the forecasted sky with
varied cubist patterns, inner-worn
labyrinths of human proximity. footpaths
and fields and playgrounds and roads
meander familiar paths over well-cropped
blades, tread and forgotten every minute,

all shades and polygons engraved on an
accurate sketching, a three-D plan of an island,
(somewhere in the middle of a sunny ocean)
weaved cell-like, measured geometry interspersed
with lines, a tempered blood system
splayed across green acres;
the face of a familiar painting.

iii.
somewhere,
an old man sits, vaguely positioned on
an ordered map; he has no place on this
canvas. ungainly joints jut
as the ground rests on him,

neither moving.
a reclusive figure beside an uncomprehending road
singular but still unnoticed
he stays unmoving as plastic hands
spin, crazily.

eyes follow the shifting, the remote prospect
of a role in the clockwork,
but not legs, however willing.

NEON REFLECTIONS

I walk a city
Where the pavements
                          pulse
Beneath my feet

I stand
Splitstreams of light
Below me
Crossing bridges, spanning distances
Measured only by time, experience and memory.

I walk a city
Which unfurls before me
A gorgeous vari-colored tapestry
Diamond-bright cocktails
In the satin sheen of dusk
A technicolor bright neon stain
Velvet tumble of unending parties
In a vodka-blurred gin haze
Fashionable cafe society on a high-gloss carousel
All day-glo dazzle and ultra-violet glamour
My spinnaker wheel
                    shoots off
                          sparks

As I whirl through this landscape
With Dionysian abandon
Head tilted back
Against the jewelled rush of traffic
Kiss of wind on my skin
With its siren song of endless promise
        and infinite glittering possibility.
A heady tide of wild sweetness
Breathing in champagne distilled in air

I spin yet faster
Gather speed
      Momentum builds
Frenetic radiance bright enough to blind
Keening sharp
Crystal about to shatter
Laughter rising to a scream.
A gilded carousel with a hollow centre
Gaiety razor-edged
      with despair

An aerial moon
      Hovers
Suspended in silvered tranquillity
          above
a city that I walk
      Seeking to forget
when every detail speaks of you
      Seeking to forget
the floodlit wash of incandescent memory
      Seeking to forget
this city that has long since

 ceased to be mine.

GREY AND WET IN SINGAPORE CITY

It's only five o'clock
but it feels like seven
spots of water appear on the car window
purportedly falling
falling
falling
from grace, from the clouds

The man over there
sacrifices his umbrella's aridity
to save his own
I hear the proverbial pitter-patter on the car roof
as we rush by
He withdraws into himself

The girl at the street lights
holds *Time magazine* over her head
did she think to spite the weather
by not carrying the sacrifice?
Or is she too young to understand?
At least seventeen
Seventeen minutes before I'm late for my music lesson

Construction workers
resigned as they are to getting wet
squat, watching us
watching me
in the dry white car
speeding
on a wet grey road

If I go here go there
everywhere there's radio
but not for the old woman
she's outside

with her shopping
they're all outside
outside with the grey and the wet
outside

They're all
sullen
separated from the next person
by a three-foot wall of water and air
and greyness
and I'm
dry
very dry
dry as a fly in July
but they're wet
very wet
wet as a jet in Phuket
and I'm
reading
my books before we get there
or get
into trouble with the teacher
who looks a lot like that old woman

Rain in Singapore
gives us new social strata.

SATURDAY EPISODES

Churning sea-river, seamlessly flowing,
tunnelling their way from area to area. The
lightning-blistered sky gives no worry to their
guardian structures beneath a raging land.
Hand holding hip, a finger entwined
stopping to exchange pleasant smiles and
kisses on the brief escalator ride.

When I'm on my way home they're there again,
off the escalator. Rear bus seats and the
panel of the train they're in awkward
positions. I just sigh, forming vapour puddles
on the windows, and listen to some song
on my discman.

THE HEART OF THE CITY

seven, in the evening.

the birds twitter their last undulations
but the city is yet laid to rest.
along the roads cars whizz up and down
like thoughts, here and then gone in a flash, in
a pile of dust, that scatters itself over
tangerine lights that hang ripe over the concrete,
and red apples and green apples at the crossroads

so that, when we stand high above the world
watching the blood of urban life pump itself —
left right, left right, by traffic lights
we see nothing more than an apple or two in
a dusty tangerine concrete grove
with thoughts that are gone in a flash;
they hardly make much sense.
my mind whizzes, twizzes, and turns;
i grip the window sill and look down, knuckles white.

watch the ant-people scurry past one another,
happy and contented, with no questions, no answers,
tunnelling deeper into the heart of the city.

THE HANGING PEOPLE

A breathing body rides this train,
its single hiss dies.

Into a wailing bend tracks turn,
rooted to purpose.

They halt at a
certain place
where a short-lived wind leaves
in the rolling thunder of closing doors.

Watching clocks with tired eyes,
they pass on to the next stop, the next stop
that has left before they arrive.

They do not know what they long for,
rest provides no answer.
Stumbling after lost time,
they clutch after handle rings —

the hanging people wait and wait
have never seen an end
do not recall how to learn by questions,
and know only of answers

SCIENCE PARK DRIVE

for Howard

He would travel all the way to the end
And he never complained although the M I s passed
Him by, so one bus-driver every day
Performed the charity of stopping. Thus
He boarded, loosely swayed with every bend
Or squeezed between the cheap colognes of last-
Rank executives, and never, when push gave way
To shove, resisted. If showers came to pass,
He leapt on patchworked, no umbrella in hand;
The floor became a smudge of watered dust.
All this because, unreally, day by day,
He dropped to listen to each trivial fuss
Cooked up by consumers who misapprehend
Sales talk by default, each indignant blast,
Each change of diskettes, each long-winded bray,
Each compliment. He tried his working-class
Set, ear-pieces and e-forms to transcend,
Till voices grumbled through his sleep, like rust
On old nails, and dead tones led his nerves to fray,
Till in his dream he saw the evening bus.

from WORK

All morning the rattle of
newspapers, the thick smell
of cheap coffee that shakes
you awake slowly. Small
petty units of time slip by
uncounted, and are lost
forever. What passes for work,
passes, until the time comes

to pretend to give it all up
and make a break for it. Five
minutes after five p.m. you're out
in the car park, waiting for the bus
that will take you away from
all this, the same chair and table
you'll have to come back to
tomorrow. But not yet.

If you haven't dozed off you see
through smudged glass and tired
eyes, the road unwinding behind
you at fifty kilometres per hour,
if you can pull away from the rush
hour traffic that threatens to eat you
up, to pull you into itself, and never let go.

Heave past the light factories, sour
and black with grease, the heavy vehicle
park, where construction vehicles, their
tires and tracks caked with dried mud
are lined up row by row in a way
that makes the tall grass think of earth —

crushed, opened, bared, discarded —
and fear the worst.

At the traffic lights, time rumbles to a stand-
still, pausing for breath, before it shovels
all the waiting cars forward to wherever
they were headed. The air buzzes
with secret clockwork, the years left
to the contract you signed with yourself,
until you'll let yourself live. So many minutes
left until the wheels stop,

and you call yourself home. The ground
beneath you, which you've never stooped
to smell or feel, since childhood, swells
with new growth, even as you pass over it.
Leaves of grass
survive the monthly trimming of the field;
their gaunt fingers point cleanly to sky,
counting down the hours of daylight.

END OF SHIFT

The day has been too long.
I leave the building
Looming large and white
Like a twenty-four hour termite queen
Still churning in her bowels.
I'm glad to show her my tired back
And if I were able to, would've
Enjoyed doing something
Rude in her face.
But I only have spirit enough
To get me to the last
Bus home.

It takes forever
But it arrives growling.
I mumble my fare to the driver
In Mandarin (I am a loyal citizen)
Evoking a few tired smiles from
A few who can still work their faces —
I hadn't noticed the driver's Indian.
He thinks I'm, being funny
And jerks the bus to life
Throwing me scowling into
The dead innards of the
Metal monster.

Comfort is a state of collapsed inertia
With the wind blowing away the day
From my mind.

The bus hurtles in the dark.
Tomorrow morning
Is a concept alien as work to me right now.
The bus hurtles in the dark
And the wind mercifully blows the day
Away from my mind.

EVENING

Nothing but a silence like still mountains,
distilled from a day full of nothing but sun
and hard bustle. Trees, blooming like fountains
of calm, water the pavement with shade. On
every street, a mute choreography
of lamps shake off darkness, putting on light.
Nothing but stillness, and the whispered, shy
conversation of leaves into the night.

Allow yourself this moment, this brief space
of hours. Taste evening in its difference,
its newness: the clean wash of a bright place;
isles of quiet. Thankful for the absence
of day, you take in skyline, the landscape
of relief, cool thoughts, feelings of escape.

outside it's just

outside it's just another
sit in cafés laughter evening
with a movie on the way midnight
as the sun bounces blue off
skyscraping silver screens
good guys gun girls goodnight
goodnight a thousand times goodbye
a whole load of good
riddance to the real world
so nice it would be so
but what about the girl at home
in the shattered minute of
a thousand pills spilling still
unbleaching her tongue
tired under a running tap
while cotton stains 100% white
her angry wrists undying
desert in her throat parched nose
on fire burning burning
as *shantih* tried to come in
through the window but broke
the glass pain instead cutting
itself sudden dead burning
so she thinks she would get out
since no one can get in
parental wire barbed secure
till a daughter's love and marriage
shitting horse and bloody carriage
while outside the other world under
green umbrellas smoking caffeine eyes
rove over cute furries
run of the hiroshima mill
and wearily close themselves tight
to the consequence of her eye
in a blue light on a cab

her heart packed in bags at her feet
trying to fly 2 a.m. of a brand new day
as the silicon smiles of plastic people
gaily drunk on swirling cubes
of melting life hang over
hatred of a screaming loneliness
and each superficial pleasure from
hand on knee in hair between lips
her fist trembles in her mouth speeding
to nothing she knows everything
she wants oh sweet freedom
undying beyond the shattered minute
of pills bleach razors broken window
to a hello hanging on dawning sun
out on the streets now
she's inside just another
sit in cafés laughter morning
with a movie on the way midnight
a whole load of good
riddance to the real world
so nice it would be so
but what about the girl at home
contemplating to sleep perchance to
dream of the outside streets
her eye on a blue light escape

AN EMPTY CINEMA

After the movie, an empty cinema,
A hundred park benches planted in neat rows,
The furniture for escape,
The clear sweat of girls and boys
Holding hands or popcorn boxes
Sticky on the arm-rest
But you stare ahead into the distance
And wonder at the whiteness of the screen
Where a paradise of images was last seen
Behind the curtain
By the warmth of the still huffing projector.
The closing credits bring you to earth
In another bumpy, unedited sequence of your life.

NOSTALGIA

Walking back
to this old part of the city
where the shophouses and
the five foot ways
smell so much of
new paint
over it.
Childhood memory lanes are
evocatively vogue
bathing in neon now.
Don't give me
a double dose of nostalgic chic
through the espresso steam
filling my nose.
I really love the feeling
of strong coffee
in my mouth
for what it is.
Don't make me drunk
on the good, old days.
I'm only here to savour
the frosty gulps of
designer beer.
Let me
gyrate in my hip retro gear
through the night
without so much as
clinging to the past.

SOMERSET BAR

candlewax trip
on a drip
    drip
       double
            tip
      tipping
         peanut shells
downa frothing sax
track and all
      that jazz,
           jive
  swing a wink
a while,
     watch
me smile
    swaying
to the thum
      drum
your happy fingers
          sing,
     ringing
sweet music   ah
      lah
    dee
   dah
to my
     ears.

STAINED GLASS, MARINA BAY

urban nightfall
skyscrapers in still silence
speckled light patterns
glance off walls of windows
shifting steadily
in the moon's unsteady flow

rhythms of the dark
waft
along the waterfront
across the waves
to rest on jagged rocks
before the tide turns

a bottle dances on the water,
clinks against the crumbling seawall,
bobs out
then slips back
into oblivion
amidst an untidy clump of debris,
an amorphous blight
on sleek stainless steel sheen

mirror on stained glass:
traces of a fresh morass?

FINGERS OF THE CAPE

I rise in a phantom city
where a dark veil hangs careless,
merging with star-whispers.
Miracles of moonlight dart,
choke the shadows.

Sprawled on oozing fingers
of the Cape, the City,
a child's unfinished jigsaw puzzle
is cast-about, dishevelled.

Open the petals of night,
drink from the nectaries.

> Only the moon is real.
> We are broken shadows
> of giants and old gods.
> Even the owls hooting
> are sounds and shadows,
> dew-drops sleeping
> are thoughts and shadows:
> only the moon is real.

Where the dark veil hangs careless
merging with star-whispers
the sum-total is a phantom city.

SINGAPORE NIGHT SONG

Where no owl cries its kill above city blocks
and the moon does not dominate
a night landscape
stars are as bright as street lights allow.

Headlamps and metal colours,
horns and exhausts, car bumpers:
The traffic is the only other animal awake.

Walk past the Merlion,
spotlighted to an edifice,
feel beneath shows, sidewalk trees shrug
off cement with roots,
and outside the concert hall,
where no concert is being staged,
hear the american top ten
spill from a walkman.

You know, nearby, people
relish a bite of satay
and maybe a walk after,
that the sun over telephone wires
and sparrows with their gutter songs
will eventually come;
but neither horizons nor thrushes.

If you cannot learn to love
(yes love) this city
you have no other.

NIGHTFALL

an earthbound angel longing for home
gazes at a road sign that points to the sky

among the entanglements of confessions and lies
clandestine lovers find each other side by side

under a streetlight a man in black waits
for that one rain to wash away his life

a child with searching eyes swings herself higher
before taking one last drag from her dying cigarette

meanwhile
the whole world sleeps
restless in our dreams
awake in our beds.

PAST MIDNIGHT

I turn the light on to see if I am still there.
The bulb creeps to life, resentful
at being roused to work. The dreary repertoire
which a discordant band went through a dozen times
during a neighbour's funeral, are marching
in my head. I hum a classical tune, summon
the words of a sentimental song
to expel the stubborn band. The blaring trumpets
cut them down with a single blow.

Life is perpetual unrest
in the housing estates. The endless knockings,
the stampeding feet, the hurricanes of bad temper,
the eternal television, the thrashing bodies,
the endless rituals of life and death.
Where is the point of stillness
art directs us to?
My mind veers crazily.
I turn the light off.
The bulb goes on burning inside.

THE WAY THINGS ARE

i.
6 a.m.
Lightning shivers in the spaces
between skyscrapers.
I can see it all through the rain-speckled
window of the bus I'm in;
hurtling comfortably toward heaven
on the arched back of Benjamin Sheares,
navigating by the constellations of lights
in the city centre.

This is not so much a place as a pause
between moments, as easily shattered
as the silence before the next word is spoken.
Such words as are uttered
by the signposts that I see now as I pass;
one for every one of us,
populating this island like a second race.
There is a chosen people on the edge
of a new land, two geographies
engraved on their foreheads forever:
this is who we are,
this is where we have come from
and where we are going.

ii.
Tanjong Pagar is a soundscape
of steel creatures colonising our shores.
Speaking a skeletal roar, what they disgorge
by day and night streams forth
in early traffic forever.
These are some thoughts at the tail-end
of a millennium: the same thoughts that perhaps
inhabited the old shophouses huddling elbow to elbow
on the edge of this river as they watched
every sunrise and setting of a century.

Tomorrow
they will be whitewashed houses
indolent in the sun. But for now,
there is only the slow dismantling of our lives
from the inside, until all that will be left
are the street-lights disembodied
above the trees, and morning rain
falling lightly over the city.

DRESSING

Halfway into your blueshirt,
You whisk dreamless conversations we never had
into self-inflicted wounds of words,
rayon textured, spun dry and hung
midway between the sky and my periwrinkles.
I watch intently, hooknosed and sharp-beaked,
planing at every crease my iron forgot,
planning the day's grocery list from your frowns,
and, still, mussing your hair, I left —
A fleeting shadow across mine and your picture
hung across a cross of drapery you called feminine.

Tie-knot slips. And you are back to square one,
redressing intimacies that should stranger us;
the act — a hungered top-heavy bereavement,
from absentminded ice-cubed trays, empty
to accusing toilet seats, left standing indignant.
Eyeing you, I ease your slippered foot,
hardcased in pigskin leather, evening brushed
leavened with rising morning expectations
and now, dropped cruelly.

You do a quick half-step, missing tabletops,
missing my upturned lips, you blow into them :
a soft acquiesce, imprinting airwise, love.
I will pull the door's handle and let you go.

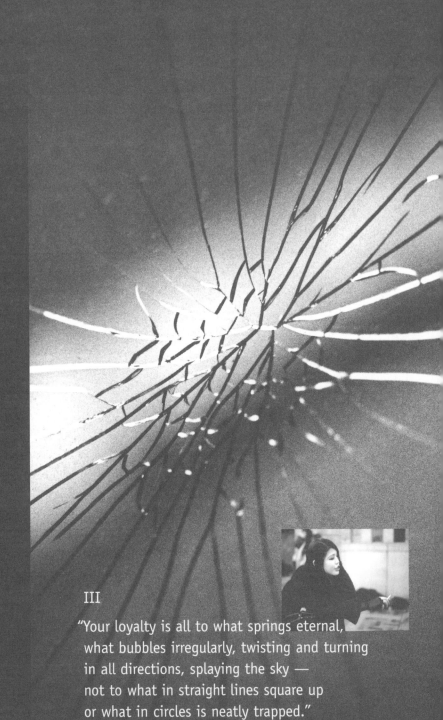

III

"Your loyalty is all to what springs eternal,
what bubbles irregularly, twisting and turning
in all directions, splaying the sky —
not to what in straight lines square up
or what in circles is neatly trapped."

SELF-PORTRAIT

This morning I thought I ran out of toothpaste.
A panicked squeeze saved the day. I hate change.
Change is when my voice slips an octave when I switch language.
Change is that empty feeling watching a bad TV show finale.
Yet I work hard at straddling two worlds. Feels schizophrenic.
I have a one track mind; it slides in and out easily. I'm willing
to compromise. I am hairless. Someone said I was too pedantic.

I looked up the word. I'm of the opinion that life's
greatest comedies are tragedies. What I said was very Greek,
but I am no alpha male. I trusted Myers-Briggs,
perhaps too much. I feel I've become a caricature of myself.

I remember last night's dream now: I was arranging
the middle initials of the last three women
I kissed. It spelt "EMU".

LOSING IT

I think I lost me midsentence in a supermarket aisle while reading
with disbelief my list of ingredients and nutritional facts.
I had said I was too old to ride the trolley but ended up following a
different me in the same dress buying different things at the same prices.
Already I have begun to forget the exact details of what I was
wearing and how I smelt. I have called out my name on the intercom but no-one has come
save for a queue of lost children I don't know who are also waiting
for their names. One of them handed me his IC number; I said thank you.

I think I lost me somewhere between Aisles Two and Infinity. I'm not
so careless as to get lost from the beginning. I have crawled to the top
shelf so I can see everyone and no-one can see me
but they have seen me, and before I see their faces I'm selling out.
Of course I am touched, but I wonder where the money is going.

Please come home,
I'm waiting.
Dinner is cooking and it's something I like.
While stocks last.
We accept plastic.
Tomorrow afternoon we're having free samples.
Maybe you mispronounced
my name
and I never knew you were talking to me.

If you see me,
Remember to tell him, at least,
that I miss me.

AUTOBIOGRAPHY

Like most of us, I can't remember how
I was separated from my first love.
(Did it die, did I break it, was it stolen
Or did it fly out through the open window?)
I didn't have radio-tuning parents
Who filled the house with music
Or instilled in me "a love of the cinema".
I never recalled my mother coming home
From the hairdressers' with a new hairdo
Or father teaching me fishing, or
Staying up to watch football on TV.
He did once bring a kite home but hung it
On my bedroom wall (he turned it into
a portrait, it wasn't his fault the wall
never became more of a sky). Meanwhile
Cousins came for visits wearing braces
And chattering about comics, bicycle scars,
And camping out, ghost stories (don't tell
that one, tell the one where Daddy used
the torchlight and Mummy screamed and dropped
her things and laughed like a hyena). We drank
Boiled water in the house, and sometimes
Waking from a nap I would wander the rooms
To find mother copying cross-stitch designs
From a book or father watching a subtitled
Chinese re-run. So I slept again, dreaming
Of playing toys away from the sunlight
That leaked in between hawk-eyed curtains
Gold-plating afternoon dust to shining pollen.
When I awoke I was twenty, being asked
If I had a happy childhood. Yes, the one
We all have: filled to the brim
With the love of absent things.

LETTER FROM BEDOK REFORMATIVE TRAINING CENTRE

Remember when you taught me how to
play *congkak*? Moving the marbles and seeds from
hole to hole? Do you understand now? All those days
when I was missing; when I hit the streets to roam,
all I was trying to do
was to find my own way home.

up & down

for the past one hour
i have sat here
watching you

walk up and down
        up and down
                        up and down

in your ragged clothes
your stenchful mouth
 your barefeet dire...

drinking my coffee
you make me ask
where you fit in

where in this urban landscape
can you

walk up and down
        up and down
                        up and down

without raising questions

SIDEWALK PUNK

Dedication to an Orchard Road fanatic

wimp smile take a bow say hello wave goodbye take
a swig of the cigarette
taste of tobacco in your mouth lack of inspiration
life sucked out
and you continue to smile,
mouth wide open with fly trooping in and
you swallowing hard as you take another
swig of that cigarette
that's filtered but none the less dirty and unpure —
just like you
and i think, hypocrite, who are you to
tell me what to do with my life or stare at me that way,
with your eyeballs jutting out as if cerebro-spinal fluid had
erupted into your sockets as your brain leaked
rationality into what you saw
your spine curving as gravity weighed down upon you with its
10 newtons whilst your little crotch
      balanced
those flabby cheap down town shop branded cargo jeans a miracle
that they
don't
fall
down.
i'd hang my hand and flaccid arm around your shoulder,
shaking you naming you screaming at you calling you "friend"
had i not realized that you're a loser,
just like the rest of them —
opposites of wimps we'd like to tag
          label
           extinguish
          diminish

IRONY

i.
The cap was Boy London,
The belt was Emporio Armani.
Valentino adorned the legs,
And Ray-Bans shielded the eyes.

Cologne was distinctly Drakkar Noir,
Had beautifully conditioned hair anytime, anyplace.
The watch was a Tag, or perhaps no cracking under pressure.

His boots were Doc Martens, or
                    Yellow Cabs
That carried him around.

            So he walked up to me, and, smiling,
                    His breath smelt like French Cuisine.
                He asked:
                    朋友，请问厕所
                    在哪里?

ii.
The cap was K-mart,
The belt was Giordano.
Lawman adorned the legs,
But no shades…

Cologne was something I borrowed from Dad,
Uncle Raju did a very neat cut for $5.
The watch was a Tag, or perhaps I would just ask people.

My shoes were Ogaan, or
                    Bata
That carried me around.

            So when he walked up to me, smiling,
                    My breath smelt of Cuppage Western food.
                    I answered
                            "I'm sorry, I don't understand you, I
                            spent most of my life in America.

THE @ GENERATION

"Starting today you are a brand ... you're every bit as much a
brand as Nike, Coke, Pepsi, or the Body Shop ... writing your
own Mission Statement to guide you as CEO of Me, Inc."
~ Tom Peters, Fast Company

My mobile phone generation,
In contact but beyond reach,
A hunger gnaws between their narrowed eyes
Offering regular joss-sticks of time and pay,
Before the alter of sodium-lit brand-names.
Survivors of the struggle for status,
Only ever lived in a garden city of peace and plenty
Surrounded by neutral jungle country.
Never seen the Merlion roar,
Seduced by slick images of war
Projected on giant multiplex screeens.

My generation of math and science prodigies
Excel early in memorising and mesmerising
But wane in their twilight twenties
With unimaginative excuses for their uncreativity.

My generation has not Acquired Immunity to Desire and Sex,
From the lure of younger sisters
Sporting kamasutra crop-tops
Showing off smooth, flat stomachs
And the dimple of a pierced belly-button,
Encouraging the navel-gazing
Of a whole generation of men.

My shopping, job-hopping, clubbing, hubbing, hot-mailing
Futures-trading, techno, web-surfing @ nowhere generation
Could be dying of the wrong lifestyle
But will wear the right brand to the fat-free end.

GRAFFITI IN THE LADIES

In the privacy
of this public lavatory
someone has purged
herself of her oppressors
and stereotypical docility:

for the Emperor of Japan
to Indira Gandhi,
and underlings in between;
PMs, MPs, the lot —
all called to judgement
in torturous outpouring:
sentenced for crimes,
nepotic dynasties, taxes,
arrogance, brutalities,
even sexual excesses,
as crudely enumerated
as mind-boggling.

You hear a voice
too freedom-bound to shut up
in its executions.
The warped calligraphy
is like a dance of death;
she prefers to strip herself
for solitary audiences
whose responses she may anticipate,
the place's ambience being
safe, accommodating frame.

You wonder if it's shock or shame
that you feel. Or maybe both.

It's easy to say
someone *hysterical* did this.

Does violence have a gender?
Has woman been clapped so much in her place
she has no room to face her demons
but the public lavatory?
Surely this vandalizing speaks much more
than the writing on the wall?

GRAFFITI CONVERSATIONS

To judge from the maze of felt-tipped, lead
And inky scrawls, a world's gripes emptied
Down three sides, the most private of public
Places is where noughts and crosses joust.
Enter at your own risk: a toilet
Strewn with unflushable anons:

HOW COME MOST ANTI-ABOBORTIONISTS ARE MEN?
A woman has to live with her choice forever
and all you do is cause more pain for her by condemning her
YES, and World population growth is out of control
Every abortion destroys a human life
MURDER the BLOODY ABORTIONISTS

VOTE WOMEN WHO WANT TO BE CHICKENS!

Slogans strike their half-remembered chords:

Out, out brief candle
SUBVERT THE DOMINANT PARADIGM
WOMEN OF THE WORLD UNITE
New world order same old lies

Free advice as
for a good time wring 4689055 and ask for Mark Twist

Prompts swift reproach —

For something better why not try 7869505?

Someone has inscribed

BELIEF IN GOD IS THE END OF ALL SORROW

        sitting, leaning, standing, one should guess
But another bans heavenly trespass:

*On the contrary human selfishness
Is the cause of all sorrow*

Surely not. Sweeping voices
Squeeze this silent scream —

*Retile this cubicle
I want to shit in peace*

Indeed; these ablutions spar from tile to door
Rebound between planes, pull back or forward
Unloading the present with the departed;
Only the floor stays clean.
Who says going to the toilet is mindlessly physical?
It's when you're most vulnerable
And at your ease that inhibitions
Count for least —

Get better pens: I can't read your comments

MEETING POINT

The unchanged meeting place waits
still with the constancy of years

Strangers to each other's everydays,
we embrace: exchange hearts, extend
familiar warmth, smiles, a laugh
I have missed for months.

The unchanging crowd through
Wisma Atria has not yet trodden out
our past, hidden away in Famous Amos
cookie jars. Our stops for Free Smells
and coincidental acquaintances remain
bottled and crisp.

These white-floored, air-conditioned
Streets, home to gaps of years in which
we were, became, perhaps still are.

We take lifts and escalators the way
we have been e-mailing messages;
alphabet trains transporting love across pagers.
It is still Paolo's for Duck Pizza, coffee
for more hours outside of indecision
contemplating time.
We used to say we waste ourselves —
waiting.

It is still the same.
We cannot wait anymore to speak
in ways that have not changed
outside of who we are.

STOCK EXCHANGE

We gesture,
Fingers lifting, motions
Rising in a flurry
Of buy. Sell. Close deal.

These words, more substantial
— My fingers reach across the table, touching yours —
Than words themselves
Speak across the distance.
And I say you say
— Your fingers squeeze mine —
That there is something between us
When there is nothing
Between our palms.

We barter and bandy these stock phrases
— Free. Keep. Tonight. Buy. Sell. —
With actions of flesh, moving in a dance
Not unlike the intricacies trading
On the floor.

Our hands, moving caricatures
Of still frame images
Sketch a play of words within
A canopy of sky skyscraper grey,
Across a stage of air.

'ALLO 'ALLO

To an unhearing eye,
the man on a cell phone
is wired unto his own —

muttering at length
to a mute voice,
his medium's hand miming home a point —

he's at once absent and absurd,
disconnected as the insane and saints
who too hear a calling in their heads.

"TRY AGAIN LATER"

"We regret to advise that
the person at extension 4..2..6
is not at her station.
Please leave a message
or try calling again later."

Later.

"We're sorry, the person at extension 4..2..6
is not at her station. At the beep, you may :
press 1 to leave a message, or
press 2 for more options.
Alternatively, you may wish to try calling again later."

2.

"You have selected 2 — "more options".
Please press 3 to speak to an operator, or 4 to hold.
Alternatively, you may wish to try calling again later."

3.

"You have selected 3 — to speak to an operator.
We're sorry, all our operators are busy at the moment.
Please hold the line and we will attend to you shortly.
Alternatively, at the beep, you may :
press 1 to leave a message, or
press 2 if you wish to revert
to your desired extension.
Alternatively, you may wish to try calling again later."

2.

"We regret to advise that
the person at extension 4..2..6
is not at her station.

At the beep, you may :
press 1 to leave a message, or
press 2 for more options.
Alternatively, you may wish to try calling again later."

2.

"You have selected 2 — 'more options'.
Please press 3 to speak to an opera .."

3.

"Hello, Operator?"
"Yes?! Can I hep-chew?"
"I am looking for Miss Mary Lim.."
"What extension?"
"Extension 426, but .." "Hold on ah"

". We're sorry,
the person at extension 4..2..6
is not at her station.
At the beep, you may :
press 1 to leave a message, or
press 2 for more options.
Alternatively, you may wish to try calling again later."

1.

"This extension is not
recording any more messages
because the mailbox is full.
Please press 2 for more options.
Alternatively, you may wish to call again later."

click.

RAPUNZEL WAITING

I stand at my window,
framed by bars, looking out
into the sunlit land. Outside,
the tree is quiet
watching me through worm-eaten leaves
and the darting mynahs gleam blackly
like an old woman's eyes

it is only three storeys down,
but my hair only reaches my shoulders
so I turn instead to the computer
and press the Get Mail button,
stretching the capability of
an infinite braid of optic cables
trying to summon
you.

IRC

sexygirl enters the room.

> HI!!!!! choruses of exuberance
> harlowe! a cheerful greeting

(silence)

cuteboy enters the room.
cuteboy tells sexygirl, > ARLOE!
sexygirl is pleased (don't shout it's rude)
> hey! long time no see!
> did you hear about lisa?
> she went out with "jason"...
> turns out he's a she (oh, poor dear)
serves her right :)
> *grin*
> LOL
> ROTFL
> LMAO
> ROTFLMAO

sexygirl leaves.
cuteboy leaves.
> Goodbye.

3AM ON IRC

for Peter on IRC

on the screen before me
your words fall like raindrops

on a windowpane. my own
windows are closed to muzzle

the ceaseless whisk of automobiles
that seem to make the night

more transient than it is.
buses trundle, their yawning hulls

as empty as lanterns.
rear-view mirrors catch

the glimmer of eyes
at the ends of their wicks.

it is a night meant for suffering.
the stars stun like cigarette burns

on the back of a slave.
but you came on-line,

and your words fall like raindrops
on the hard salt of my night.

there is kinship in sadness.
joy is a sole pair of dancing shoes

up for grabs, but sorrow
is the yoke that binds

even as it weighs down our human heads.
and when you spoke of being in love

how urgent revelations showed:
that the habit of loving

is our one and only shot at happiness.
nobody regrets for having loved,

even the wrong people, or in wrong doses,
because we remember how it once stood for right.

tonight the drizzle of traffic
is drowned by the torrent of your words.

IN CONVERSATION

I laugh
And I say
You speak
You are enigmatic and don't know it.

Talk to me. Let me hear you
Say out loud who you are
Not, and who you are.
Let me cast my words,
Like the oracles of old,
Into the wind of
Breathless smiles and
Soundless sighs.

Somewhere across the land
You hear me. Start
And stop a part of my pattern.
I seem to receive all
You tell me, while

You speak of yourself as
Someone that you are
Transcending the pauses,
Stops and clicks of morse code
That I translate in synapses
Hearing you pause
In meaning, meaning a pause.

Let me muse on you,
Ruminate on truths half
Illuminated in the afterglow
Of love we build
In ponderous silences
through this mortal coil.

WHAT THEY TALK ABOUT IN THE BEDROOM
WHEN THE CHILDREN ARE FAST ASLEEP

A poem to be read in a whisper

"I don't think she fails on purpose."
"Nowadays my knees can tell me when it's going to rain."
"Do you think they're asleep yet? I can hear them giggling."
"You know our neighbours threw away their plants? Even that tall Japanese bamboo."
"What was that?"
"Would you like to go to KL this December? We could buy you some scarves."
"Just now your sister made comments about our kitchen."
"Why do you always wake up in the middle of the night to go to the bathroom?"
"Just now I forgot to bring in the slippers when they washed the corridor."
"It's nothing, someone threw a bottle down the rubbish chute."
"Did you have to beat him so hard?"
"Do you think if we had a house like that we'd be happy?"
"Ever since I married you there's been nothing but money problems."
"Your aunt has lost so much weight, I wonder how she did it."
"I worked at the floors since morning, can you smell the Dettol?"
"Admit it, you love your son more than your daughter."
"Who were you talking to on the phone just now?"
"Don't talk facing that side. I can't hear you."
"Don't touch me like that."
"Can you hear me like this?"
"I need sleep. I can't sleep. I need my sleep."
"Goodnight. Goodnight."
"Wake up, wake up, I think I hear something."
"That was me."
"That wasn't you. What are you saying?"
"No, that was me, yes."

A SON'S CONFESSION

During one of their rare
outings together, Eric told
his father that he was 'gay'.
The older, heavily-wrinkled
man repeated the word, playing
with it on his lips, an etymologist
positing its semantic possibilities.
Seeing that his father did not
fully understand, Eric provided
further clarity and offered,
"'Homo'? 'Faggot'?"
And dark understanding rose
to the surface of his aged face
by way of a frown, deepening
the lines on his forehead. They
were strolling along the corridors of
a mall and the noise of bustling shoppers
became a distraction from having to listen
to the silence which was hardening
between them. Finally, Eric
mustered the courage to ask, "So, Pa
what do you think?" Father did
not reply. It seems, according to Eric,
they have stopped talking since.

MRT ANTAGONISM

Humming.
We hear... Loud.
Buzzing, buzzing ... buzzing.

That woman in the corner with the maroon.
Decrepit.
                    Umbrella-like.

She exudes this *ish*ness.

Undefinable.

Encroaching on my sphere.
Buzzing wildly.

Comatose in the corner ... maroon-ish.
Motionless.
                    In an invasive way.

These days we argue from silences.

ROSARY

I'm sitting next to a girl counting beads on her rosary while a hard
industrial house track plays in my head. As she counts, the walls of the
train crumple and collapse, and the sound of twisted metal rings through the
carriage in time with the beads passing along the string. As the walls fall
away, the glass windows scrape and smash against the tunnel sending shards
of glass flying across the carriage and onto the track. The girl keeps
counting, and I just watch her.

The train hurtles along the track going faster and faster but everything
looks like it's in slow motion. The track in my head pounds faster and harder
but my heart and breathing slow down to a whisper. And everyone is either
checking their watch, reading a paper, looking impatient or asleep. The girl
is still counting. I think I like her. I think I'd die for her.

The apocalypse happened inside my head while everyone was on their way to
work. The world ended, or at least could have, but nobody noticed, or did
anything different. All those dreams, ideals and ambitions in a single
carriage that could have been unfulfilled. Nobody noticed the splinters and
shards of glass in my eyes.

ON AN MRT TRAIN

She sits across me on the crowded train
Reading, trying to read her Chinese paper,
Its bright red characters leaping out
From the front page news and spilling
Over onto the colourless floor,
Her light brown face shrouded by her
Grass-green, age-old head scarf
Folded neatly, melting into the folds
Of her long bright dress.
Her dress and scarf provide the frame
For which she is the portrait,
Her life in between
Chinese characters grasped by
Hands which fast and pray
Five times a day,
And worship in a different tongue,
Her living portrait an unsurprising picture
(The red words on the front page arrest
More eyes than she)
Among other beings in between
MRT stops, and the signposts
That mark invisible territory,
Unknown lines of experience.
What, after all, separates Outram Park
From Tanjong Pagar except a two-minute journey?
What divides the bright red words
From the hands which refuse food once a year?

Her stop comes, and she leaves,
Leaving, accidentally, her newspaper
For others to read,
For others to take her place aboard this crowded train.

MEMORY

It was her face — pouched, sagging,
lined and traced with threaded age.
Or perhaps it was her eyes —
tattooed twice; scratched and marked
for past reference in a fast fading world.
She stood before me, filled with the
scent of passing; she forced me to look.

And all at once I was called back

to grey void decks and narrow corridors,
where the drift and glow of incense
strikes the porcelain Buddha on a red altar.
The neighbour, a pale boy my age,
stands outside the shuttered, shattered windows
in dirty singlet and shorts waiting to play.

Inside four rooms with patterned floors
and toothless furniture, framed photographs
hang undocumented on clean white walls.
Fish porridge is breakfast, lunch, dinner;
homework is torn from a colouring book;
and each day drips wax from untold time,
a saturated silence in hot afternoon naps.

She, without rheumatism then, clutches
my hand and calls to me in Hokkien; walks me
across the carpark to school in the morning.
He cycles back from work each evening
to play the game of hide-and-seek I always win.

It was the HDB life — dirty, arrogant,
formidable; marked by stained lifts, bamboo
poles of laundry hung out of grilled windows,
the buzz and blink of a thousand neon lights and
television sets tuned to Channel 8 turned on at night.

It was their concern — transparent, gruffly hidden,
in every toy they bought under my bidding,
every time they scolded my parents for scolding me.

But most of all, it is in the face of another
grandmother, another stranger, someone who
knows, who calls forth guilt by reminding me
of what I have so easily forgotten.

CITY GIRL'S TRIBUTE

Not yet old with wandering,
mental arthritis crippling,
still seeking modern wisdom
in modem myths, fictioning

Celtic to Chinese,
Tangsian to hybrid,
with Coke in my right,
Discman-ears plugged in;

is it a wonder
I don't clearly hear
angels rejoicing
or sighing Chang-er?

Naïve tourist untutored in traffic
(not much travell'd in realms of gold,) I sleep-
walked, fumbled amidst milkyway magic;
on magpie bridge where weaving maid alone
and cowherd were to sweet heavenly meet.
Wingéd chariots, ancient seas, nymphs, sirens
I greet in print, dream in asian ethics
remain mute not knowing how to tongue them
when I wake. I met one from far white seas
named Ulysses, claimed repute epical,
(reincarnate as monsoonal sea-beast)
had held vigil with various wanderers.
Shipwrecked, exiled, at times extolled of course,
he has lately returned as Omeros.

Meanwhile navigation sees
empires sink, islands rise,
train-traffic technologise,
ocean-air routes redesign.

With my yin-ly pulse, I map prospect commonplace
while gazing still at next waves nearing horizons,
crossing peninsulas, jotting down lines somewhere-
bound, listening to lingering music on a brink.

JOURNEYS

i.
My grandmother died when she was ninety-four,
Memory loosened, body still intact and tongue still sharp
After nine decades of significant toil,
Advancing and retreating over the tangled jumble
Of a mangled century-tossed history; closing
With the tentative, groping approach towards
The twilight door of her mind.

My grandmother died when she was ninety-four,
Born to a world of fixed geographies, unchanging histories, using
Stable compasses and proud maps that spoke only to themselves.
Why did she abandon her history-fixed future
To enter a world with no history, only an unknown future?
My history begins in the story of this young woman
And of her small uncertain steps across a crowded ocean.

The earth was bigger then, its oceans wider and deeper
And its currents more treacherous than they are now,
Carving out the stories of sundering journeys
With their mute, continuous, melancholy songs.
Hemmed in by the familiar, her world
Was only her village, her house, her people,
Surrounded by an unknown ocean of possibility and fear.

My grandmother died when I was far away.
I too have challenged the boundaries of the known
To extend the geographies of the heart and mind,
And to shake my fist at the domain of the not-yet-known,
Like her. And her journey has become a part of me;
I blur the distinctions between origins and destinations,
As she did long ago, in a journey with no end.

My grandmother died when she was ninety-four.
Ninety-four years of transgressing boundaries
To start a family that finds itself today
Crossing oceans and continents and casting dreams
On journeys much like hers,
Answering the restless urge to rise beyond the ring of hills
That encircle the story of our lives.

ii.
I scoop up the liquid stories from the ocean of her life,
But only a few hesitant drops remain,
My fingers too solid to grasp the pellucid strands
Of a life that has seen the sky open its ravening mouth
To spit fire on a wilder earth,
The traumatic nascence of a brash new nation —
Born out of wedlock and into uncertainty —
And the deaths of husband and children,
While tall buildings rose all around her,
Boldly proclaiming new truths in new tongues.

I scoop into the ocean of my history, and I draw from it
The image of a wanderer whose journey never ends
Even if he has found home, his feet touching the earth
While his heart walks the unseen paths that bear him,
Irrevocably,
Back to the ocean of shifting origins and changing sands.

Moving,
Always moving,
Always and forever changing.

iii.

What does change bring? It shatters the mirror
That only shows the misty surface of our lives
While its fragments challenge us to decipher
The unfamiliar script of our everyday journeys,
To listen to the strange rhythms that teach us,
Patiently, to remember.

iv.

To remember the living and the dead.
To remember the living smells of the funeral wreaths
And the ancestral incense swirling at my grandmother's wake,
The pungent odours mingling with the clouds of stories, dense
Amidst the chatter of reunited relatives
And the fallen petals of chrysanthemums.

To remember the living and the dead.
To remember the paths of a lone mudskipper crossing a pond,
Dancing a web of transient threads across a deceptive map,
Its feet never touching ground,
Skipping on reality even as reality dissolves
Into a liquid world without bounds.

To remember the living and the dead.
To remember the achievements of three thousand years
And the geographies of our past,
While seeking out new paths to the ever-changing ocean,
Acknowledging the falling petals of our years, yet
Creating our own reflection.

To remember the living and the dead.
To see, in the hulking towers of a hundred storeys
And in the pond of luminous lives,
And in old photographs of my grandmother's travelled face,
The testimony of irresistible time:
Our never-ending, ever-urgent chase.

V.

And so we stand, at century's end,
To pause and consider the work of man
Before it fades into oblivion:
Our footsteps on the shores of this wide ocean,
Traversing in circles, loops, endless regressions,
Yet pulled forward by the lure of the hypnotic waves,
Impelled by the brooding shadow of the encircling hills,
In this simple, cosmic dance,
A waking trance,
On these fickle, shifting sands.

The future gestures as a felt and unseen hand,
A half-hinting, seducing chameleon
That puzzles us, tempts us
Beyond the edge of any map,
Till we wander, mapless, trackless, timeless
Visionaries in an original world,
Sowers of new seeds on new soils,
Builders of bridges
Defying measure,
Across this current-tormented ocean.

ZOOMING OUT: Re-Imagining Singapore

I sit here, a cigarette in hand with an addiction-induced sense of well-being, soothed further by coffee and jazz coming over the PA. A soft rain falls; this is tropical Asia, lands of rice, bamboo and monsoon. The waitresses are arranging flowers in preparation for the after-five crowds. Baby's breath and white carnations. A touch of class for new Asians.

Two young chaps are working at the next table, speaking animatedly in Mandarin; papers scattered on table, handphone going. Modern Jazz Quartet weaves its spell. The piano cuts in. The guitar wends its way between the bass-line. Katapang and Buddha's Ficus trees form a screen around the Substation courtyard; guards against the encroaching city. This is an oasis. Outside, the city's frenetic pace pounds relentlessly. I can hear the rumble, it says that memories and sentiments are of little use, shaped, as they are, by the imperatives of economics and political will.

On one wall, which edges one side of the space, there are graffiti paintings. A frog with its tongue skewered by a baby's soother; the best of all gags! A large half-chomped apple flagrantly proclaims itself. Graphics on the walls are painted over and over again: expressions of young sentiments given free reign. Once there was a drawing of a naughty boy, now painted out, peeing near to or into a barrel. It could have been a beer barrel. A conscientious committee member of the Museum neighbour was worried that sponsors of the Substation's theatre may be annoyed, insisted that it be painted out. The Substation director protests the right to decide on such matters; threatens resignation in protest. The 'owner' of the wall asserted legal rights. The potentially offensive graphic was painted out. Art on the wall however continues, the bad taste left in the mouth fades in time, as with memories. Life goes on.

Java-teak furniture gives off a warm sense in the courtyard. Yet another touch of class. The yellow-ochre walls cast a glow-warmth for young bones cold in the light of everyday reality.

I can hear the traffic pick up. Soon, the city will empty save for the watering holes which draw in tourists and stragglers reluctant to return to cosy-land. City workers return to their little patches of precious sky making up the new towns. Life resumes at the food centres there and then they retire to watch family-life — on TV! Meanwhile the city is dead. Rats scurry across Shenton Way. An eerie silence settles over the CBD. There is no life. Will life ever come back? No city is just concrete, steel and glass. Cities need spirit and bodies to be alive. Where has the human spirit gone, to the new towns?

There are pockets of life around food and shopping centres in the city, but only eating and shopping animate them. The Tuck Shop, MPH, *char kuay teow*, *ngo hiang* at Armenian Street. The schools have all left; trailing behind the exodus to the new towns in the thirty years since urban renewal began. Raffles Girls' School, St Joseph's, Raffles Institution, ACS (Anglo-Chinese School) Coleman Street have all gone to the suburbs. The old ACS is now the National Archives, a storehouse for the debris of time.

The Modern Jazz Quartet goes on sweetly; the mandarin voices continue to punctuate the drone of the city outside, the handphones go on, lifelines to the city's pulse. Two Indian girls arrive, chat in the ruins of the abandoned transformer yard which is now part of the Substation. It too would have vanished without memory or trace had it not been for the vision of Kuo Pao Kun who had faith that ruins and the margins of everyday life constitute fertile ground for new hope to arise. So now he sits on the T21 private sector committee to help think through a new way ahead for Singapore.

He has to find how it will be possible for art and poetry to be the cradles of creativity against the canon of hard practical truth, which is money. Money that the big-spending developers of high rise office buildings will ring into the cash registers of the nation's coffers. Meanwhile, the dead city still has to wait for human life to course through its streets and to activate its squares. Only a fundamental change in the planner's land-use policies can bring life back to the city.

And so the few active places in the city are pressured by too much of life's diversity. How much sense do heavy-metal kids need when they want to vent their spleen in sound and fury at the Substation? How to risk a bust-up which may jeopardise everything there? That was Pao Kun's dilemma, but he had enough faith that somehow the risk could be managed and that the hounds of public order can be kept at bay. And his handling and faith fortunately proved adequate and right. The heavy-metal kids had their fun, knew where the risks lay, now call him "Uncle".

The rain pours, this is the tropics after all. But somehow the rain does not wash away the heavy air that sits on the city's soul. Only the pavements get cleaned. And the planners who do not know about 'air' are now frantically twiddling the knobs and pulling the levers to turn Singapore into a hub; a communication hub, a science hub, a knowledge hub, because they fear dissolution. For only the free can spontaneously re-invent themselves to face a new day; tweaking mechanical contraptions will not prevent them falling apart when the design limits of the machine are exceeded. A leaf falls on my plate, has foreign talent arrived?

An experimental experiential house was recently built in the courtyard of the Substation. It was about living; about a new way of seeing. But the exhibition was attended only by friends and a few curious visitors. Life passed it by; but something is better than nothing. Have we learnt to trim our ambitions and avert our eyes, bind our hearts? I hope we have not learnt too well.

To survive and prosper in material terms, we have become the generation that remembers to forget. We forget what is prescribed not to remember. Sure, no lies are told. It is only that the whole truth is omitted in the telling. When history is predicated exclusively on political imperatives, it is hard to see the reality for what it is. That is what Janadas Devan once said elliptically at a forum in the Substation.

A river must have a start and an end, but our view of the present reality has taken the form of discrete slices of disembodied time; sound bites in the official story line. Thus with eyes fixed on the ever-receding horizon, consciousness is locked into the perpetual present. We are thus cast adrift in the endless river of time where there is nothing with which to tie the loose ends, except fiction. Many of the young have learnt to excuse their own inaction on the grounds that they are still learning and experiencing. But who has stopped? We always act on incomplete knowledge; it is a human predicament. Walls are not just walls, they are contentions. Even allies take opposite sides to protect each other from each other. Flowers — baby's breath and carnations have become classy kitsch. They are not flowers; they are images with no fragrance.

I leave for New York on Monday, to that great sponge of foreign talent! To a New York that still succeeds because it gives enough for what it takes — that is the secret of its success.

My mind wanders over the wall and through the trees into the city. It briefly settles on the MPH nearby which has become just another bookshop, a vendor. Only the initials remain of the Malayan Publishing House, the Methodist Church's printing enterprise for bibles and other religious tracts and school textbooks. The National Library is also nearby, rendezvous for many a student, a place of fond friendships and a window to the world. Now it is to give way to a traffic tunnel proposed by engineers who cannot factor-in human sentiments. The proposition that engineering might now perhaps obey public sentiment is a new idea for the new generations. But if they knew that the Library also sits on grounds previously occupied by the British Council (where Art and sensibility in Malaya and Singapore was kindled), they would not dismiss the Malayan period as mere nostalgia. Furthermore, if they knew that the British Council had sat on the very same grounds which was once part of Singapore's first botanical garden, they would have realised that this is truly hallowed ground; link to the neighbouring farm-lands, added reason for breaking out of the agenda of forgetfulness.

In the distance, my dreaming eye sees Katong's tall swaying coconut trees (symbol of backwardness) along what was once beach, now highway. On the East Coast Park which has taken its place are dwarf coconuts made legitimate in iteration of USA's prime tropical tourism image; Hawaii. Similarly on the west coast, Pasir Panjang's villages have vanished to port expansion and condos, victims of progress. Clearly, pain has been made easier to bear when we do not remember. A long-time Malayan, Johnny Johnson, built in Pasir Panjang a resort-restaurant which conjured an ambience of outdoor tropical dining but it too fell to building regulations, which demanded concrete structures and sanitation rules. Haw Pah Villa, next door, has turned into an Americanised theme park. Chinatown is to be more Chinese than Malayan, Nanyang and the Vernacular. It is geared-up to be a piece of orientalism for the delectation of tourists. Never managing to ignite the imagination, they all failed and will continue to fail miserably because there is no ring of truth to them. They too become victims of a kind of jaded progress. Only the bold and the bright re-imagine other possibilities. Even the tourists see through the sham. The in-flight video on Singapore is embarrassing. Old warriors have too many reflexes conditioned to fight demons to take new risks including the most challenging of all; the unconditioning of their own condition.

When I speak of risks I include generosity. Not the dumb sort of hands-off giving but a smart new kind. One which sees the risks but is willing to face up to them with kindness. Only then will it be seen as sincere. Other risks include the growth of self-esteem without the need to hanker after other people's images. The young Singapore poet, Alfian Sa'at says in his published book of poems, *One Fierce Hour*, that he has lost his country to images. I know exactly what he means.

The sun casts a rosy tinge on the Carlton Hotel visible through the surrounding trees. As sun sets, a different mood sets in. Darkness shrinks space, rouses the senses, things lose definition. The imperatives of the state dissolve. The horror of the city's emptiness is averted, as eyes are drawn towards the tiny bright spots of life. The rest does not matter. As the night wears on, and as any night-bird knows, that in the progressing darkness senses sharpen; consciousness draws ever inward until finally sleep comes and phantoms are released to inhabit the vast void of inner space.

Surely every city is also Generic City. Not just a collection of artefacts, buildings, roads. Old cities have urbanism, new ones only urbanisation. Urbanism is manners married to space embodied in the fabric of the city — thus urbanism, manners, memories and ambitions are what are really important in the clarity of broad daylight. At night, urbanism is a floating world of sense and dreams. The terrors of the day recede. Rationality dwindles with the failing light. Freedom is the night; it is time to create. And in the full glare of daylight, dreams fade away again. But planners know little of this because they operate in statistics and imported images.

The so-called "new urbanism", is one of these. That it is the American new middle class' substitute for jazzed-up suburbia is not appreciated, thus it serves yet again to confuse the issue of our own urban project. That is the problem of imported images and planning bereft of living.

So we must guard against imports, learn how to live. When we avidly buy foreign talent and foreign ideas because we think they are chic, we fail to evolve what is true to our living. Urbanism is thus about freeing up our imagination about our civic urban values. The specifics of our humanity, geography and history are the grounds for real thought and creation. The Urbanism we make should be about an authentic conviviality which cuts across social classes and racial barriers, which continue to divide, polarise and bore, requiring entertainment and rules and enforcement to make life tolerable. When we are true to ourselves, our urbanism will become truly universal. No need to hard-sell our tourism. No need to hype the people into the 21st century. We will get there ourselves on our own wings. Our urbanism will not be made by the stick and the carrot.

While avowing communitarian values, it is too easy, too convenient to just place a higher value on blood and kinship ties. We need to look beyond the inner circle, to wider civic urban values. Only modern societies strive to internalise public morals into private lives within the abstract ideal of civility. Our ethnic values are thus something we need to reexamine because it is the source of our anxieties; a brake on our urbanism. People who are fearful of the unknown, and in want of hero-leaders, group and gravitate towards collective ideologies. They are amenable to authoritarian leadership. They can move mountains through hardwork and cognitive rigidity when the leadership is able. When it is not, the situation festers. Fear of being disadvantaged, being looked down upon, of losing-out, dominates our imagination even as we grow materially. When the material goal has been reached, the plateau is much more difficult to climb out of without the modernisation of the culture of everyday life. We need a lively civic urban culture to reach a new level. The grip of fear is loosening especially among the young because they are bored by the constant drum of threatening scenarios. It is time for a new imagination and a new socialisation of responsible autonomy to grow, because as the young acquire smart-work and flexible imagination, they will dream of being in other more conducive places. Only when we learn new ways of seeing and feeling will we engage our young and talented in the unfolding new world.

Making living creative and making the city liveable and lively is a new challenge for Singapore. Accompanying this must be real choices in lifestyle. The cosmopolitan centre and the conservative fringe must be allowed their differences; as it is, there is too much sameness. If a million people live in the city centre, Singapore will never be the same again. It is possible to kick-start a New Singapore. This is Singapore's predicament to resolve — equality and sameness never created creativity. This is Singapore's success story gone wrong.

There should be spatial distinctions or zones where natural differences are manifest. This is all the more necessary in a small place where even-handedness has resulted in sameness at the hands of centralised agencies. It is time to decentralise the administration for the sake of creativity. The trick is to ensure that each zone is administered and actioned separately so that each can naturally respond to, and therefore provide, distinctive styles of life and have environmental characteristics in sync with its particular locale. Indeed, differences can only come about when the milieu of each zone is different. The special quality of Holland Village is just such an example, where a unique supporting social milieu has resulted in its special ambience. But this was achieved by fluke. In a different social milieu in which we are free to gravitate to areas conducive to them, then Singapore will naturally have many different ambiences. And life will have some sparkle to it.

The city core is that special place where this can happen and where this needs to happen. Let people then chose where they want to live, to have their children educated, to work and to play. The City can become the crucible of a new creativity. It takes a smart, light touch to make it happen. Sameness deadens and is to be dreaded at all costs. And the antidotes to wealth-induced degradation are true art, scholarship and philanthropy. Otherwise, increased wealth merely feeds wants. When people want what others have in terms of tangible symbols and things, there will be sameness and intolerance towards difference. There are thus risk investments to be made with power, wealth and culture.

Boston (same size as Singapore) has 50 universities within a 50-mile radius; the Gardner Museum shines its generous spirit despite its record of scandal. Isabella Steward Gardner lived above her Museum; an heiress who knew how to live, worked to prevail against the degradation and dissolution produced by wealth. She knew of the human spirit's tendency towards corrosion — and art, intellect, scholarship and philanthropy and the feeling that duty towards others must first be gained through duty towards oneself, are the only things that can mitigate meanness and greed. Then a community of spirit will arise to give rise to a true spirit of community not needing inducements, punishments and mobilising to act in the common good. The vitality of Route 128 in Boston, a rival to Silicon Valley, testifies that scientists and engineers are not mono-dimensional creatures, they too need to breathe the fragrances provided by art and the humanities to inspire their creativity and their inventiveness.

A bit of discipline helps bolster a creative society. Discipline without sensibility confirms a society to uncreativity. Mayor Guiliani, New York's Lee Kuan Yew, puts in the discipline of late — it does good, makes the place better. New York re-invents itself once again.

Seeing ourselves is easier from a distance. We travel to see ourselves afresh. Many people however, travel in a hermetically-sealed bubble to confirm their prejudices. They see New York for its mess not its vitality. Here I am in New York City. Peeling away the images that make up our Singapore reality is like tearing away at a life of habitual thinking. But we need to start with the here and the now, and then zoom out to a different vantage point. Zooming to the past is to realise the tapestry of our time — the seams in the collage of our life; its shoring, colours, fragrances and wounds. There is so much debris and unfinished business and it should make you want to do something about it, not just soak in it. We can drown in our own consumption and our self-made iterations made bigger, brighter, louder and more.

Finally, the development of language is crucial and should be in tandem with our process of modernisation. Unless there is language to shape thought, realisations will remain vague urgings. Diction is an indicator of content in language. From the disparate peoples who gravitated to this place, a Malayan culture came about, and with it, a new voice — the Malayan voice. This voice embodied thoughts and sensibilities grown from the land inspired by a universalistic modernity, even though one part of it was focused on China, the other on the West. Nevertheless, a new sensibility arose from the rootedness in the land.

Unfortunately, as rapid modernisation took over Malayan modernity, the mechanisation of language in the nation-building years, especially in a Singapore cut off from the roots of its own modernity and its aesthetic of place, has made Singlish the orphaned child of displaced Malayanism. And so our newscasters feign an American twang. The prattle of everyday speech is cosy but unedifying — it contains no ideals.

Soon, night will fall again over the Substation courtyard and human perception will draw inwards. Will the Substation be absorbed into the Singapore night where phantoms stalk? When the Singapore Management University (SMU) campus takes its place in the city, will this bring new illumination or just add only more clamour? Will the peace be drowned out by bigger, louder, brighter, because we do not know what is "better"?

Tay Kheng Soon
February 2000, Singapore.

THE EDITORS

ALVIN PANG graduated with 1st class honours in Literature from the University of York in England. He taught for two years in a junior college and is a writer, editor and literary activist when he isn't making a living. He is involved in literary events such as the AfterWords discussion group at the Library@Orchard. He also runs a poetry website (http://poetry.s-one.net.sg). The Vice-Chairman of the Singapore Association of Commonwealth Literature and Language Studies, Alvin also assists the National Arts Council regularly in literary projects as editor, judge and events leader. A finalist in the 1995 Singapore Literature Prize Competition for poetry, his work appears in the anthology *In Search of Words* (1991), international publications such as the *English Review* and *Riding the Meridian*, and the upcoming Millennium anthology of Singapore poetry commissioned by the National Arts Council. His first volume of poetry *Testing the Silence* (1997) was launched at Singapore Writers' Week 1997 and was listed as one of the top ten books of 1997 by *The Straits Times'* Book Page. It was also nominated for the National Book Development Council of Singapore Book Award in 1998/1999.

AARON LEE SOON YONG is a lawyer and poet. His first poems were published in the anthology *In Search of Words* (1991). In the following years, his poetry was published in anthologies, newspapers and magazines in Singapore and Malaysia. He has won numerous prizes for his writing including first prize in the NUS Literary Society Poetry Competition in 1995 and third prize in the nationwide Shell-New Straits Times Poetry Competition in Malaysia. His poems have been read on national radio and television, and are also taught in schools across the country. His poetry collection *A Visitation of Sunlight* was named by *The Straits Times* as one of the ten best books of 1997. The book was also nominated for a National Book Development Council Award in 1998/1999. The following year, the title poem of his book was selected for the National Arts Council's "Poems on the Move" programme, a national initiative to bring poetry to the general public.

CONTRIBUTORS

ALFIAN BIN SA'AT is a 22 year old undergraduate at the National University of Singapore. He has published a collection of poetry, *One Fierce Hour* and a collection of short stories, *Corridor: 12 Short Stories*. He also writes plays, in English and Malay, which have been performed by The Necessary Stage (Black Boards, White Walls, sex.violence.blood.gore) and Teater Ekamatra (Causeway, Bulan Madu).

Born in 1965, BOEY KIM CHENG has published 3 volumes of poetry: *Somewhere Bound* (1989), *Another Place* (1992) and *Days of No Name* (1996). He is currently pursuing a PhD and hopes to resume work on a fourth collection of poetry soon.

CHARMAINE CHAN used to be a lawyer but left after a year of practice to devote more time to writing. She now writes for a magazine called CREAM and is a full-time journalist. She spends much time honing her craft, whether poetry or prose, and her ultimate goal is to one day publish a novel. F. Scott Fitzgerald and Truman Capote are her major influences.

CHIN WOON PING is the author of *The Naturalization of Camellia Song* (1993), *In My Mother's Dream* (Landmark, 1999) and co-author of a book of transla-tions, *Tales of a Shaman: Jah Hut Myths* (1985). Born in Malaysia, she received her higher education in Malaysia and the US. She was Senior Fulbright Lecturer in China and Indonesia, and recipient of fellowships by the Pennsylvania Council on the Arts and the National Endowment for the Humanities. Presently she lives in Vermont with her family.

FELIX CHEONG graduated from the NUS in 1990. His poems have won prizes in NUS, published in *Singa* and various anthologies and he has 2 volumes of poetry to his name. Early influences include Albert Camus and surrealist artists like Salvador Dali, but it was under the mentorship of Lee Tzu Pheng that he matured as a writer. A regular literary reviewer for *The Straits Times*, Felix is presently with CNBC Asia.

LENA CHEW recently graduated from NUS with a major in English Literature. Currently a freelance writer, she is considering a career in journalism. Meanwhile she takes time to smell the flowers with her three pet dogs, plays tennis, enjoys gastronomic delights, shops, and writes sporadically (in no particular order). She extends a special thank you to Professor Edwin Thumboo who guided her under his Creative Writing class.

GOH POH SENG was born in Malaysia in 1936. He received his medical degree from University College Dublin, and practised medicine in Singapore for 25 years. His first novel, *If We Dream Too Long*, won the Singapore National Development National Award, and has been translated into Russian and Tagalog. His other books published in Singapore include 2 novels, *The Immolation* and *Dance of Moths*, and 3 poetry collections — *Eyewitness*, *Lines from Batu Ferringhi* and *Bird with One Wing*. *The Girl from Ermita and selected poems 1961–1998* was published in 1998 in Canada, and a new book of poems will be published in Spring 2000.

GUI WEI HSIN is presently studying English at Wesleyan University in America. He finds inspiration for his writing from personal experience as well as the works of others—the poems of Robert Frost, Wislawa Szymborska, the songs of Dar Williams, Liang Wern Fook, and the musicals of Stephen Sondheim. Having acted in numerous plays, Wei Hsin believes that to enjoy poetry one should not only read, but also perform it.

GWEE LI SUI is currently a graduate student with the University of London. Among his published works are the graphic novel *Myth of the Stone* (1993) and a collection of poems, *Who Wants to Buy a Book of Poems?* (1998).

ERVIN HA is currently a doing a BBA, concentrating on Management Information Systems, at The George Washington University, Washington, D.C. USA. He cites Robert Lowell, D.H. Lawrence, WIlliam Shakespeare, William Wordsworth, T. S. Elliot, Ezra Pound as his major influences. Besides the classics, he is still thrilled by space and sci-fi books and movies, especially Star Wars. Ervin is currently working on a compilation of poems entitled "Sun Filled Underground".

A former participant and present alumnus of the Creative Arts Programme, TERENCE HENG, 22, is currently an undergraduate at the University of Nottingham reading Economics. He has published one collection of poetry and photography, *Live a Manic Existence with a Cup of Sanity in Your Hand*, and counts William Blake, AE Housman and the War Poets as some of his major influences. In his spare time, he freelances as a photographer, actor and web administrator of Quill, a literary website.

HENG SIOK TIAN writes: "It is difficult to pinpoint one poet as a dominant influence. I am drawn to specific poems by different poets and remain fascinated by Emily Dickinson and more recently Wislawa Szymborska. There's also no running away that my pursuit of English Literature as a discipline informs parts of my psyche, but so have my encounter with

Singaporean writing from Wang Gungwu's to Boey Kim Cheng's works. Perhaps it is inclusiveness that I am trying to reach at: inclusiveness of voices, verities and visions."

HO POH FUN considers T. S. Eliot, G. M. Hopkins and E. Thomas early influences, and Rilke, Pasternak, Neruda and, more recently, Szymborska, mellowing forces. *Katong and Other Poems* received an NBDCS Commendation for poetry in 1996. She particularly enjoys works on cultural, botanical and biological themes, with writings by Natalie Angier, E. O. Wilson, Thomas Friedman and Daniel Dennett heading her list of writers.

ROGER JENKINS is the Artistic Director of Dramaplus Arts, one of the most active arts education programme providers to schools. A strong drama connection is present in all his works — writing plays (*To Light A Fire* won overall 1st Prize at the 1999 Singapore Youth Festival), musicals (*Aladdin for The Kids Co* with Karen Lim) or songs (*City For The World* for National Day Parade 1998.) He relaxes by creating spontaneous stand-up comedy with The Madhatters Comedy Company.

KOH BENG LIANG, a Public Service Commission scholar, is currently doing national service. He loves reading Martin Amis and spends way too much money on CDs.

The major influences on KOH BUCK SONG's poetry derive mostly from his training in literature, which included American works especially the Modernists. Names like Seamus Heaney and Philip Larkin come to mind alongside T. S. Eliot and Ezra Pound. In his spare time, Buck Song keeps up with movies, reads less voraciously than before, tends to his garden and koi pond, and gets the bones cracking with the occasional soccer game.

GILBERT KOH CHIN WANG, 27, graduated from NUS Law Faculty and is currently a Deputy Public Prosecutor in the Attorney-General's Chambers. He enjoys good music, playing the guitar, criminal law and psychology. Favourite writers include Charles Bukowski, Ernest Hemingway and Raymond Carver. He was shortlisted for 1997 Singapore Literature Prize, and a few of his poems have been previously published in *Singa*.

KOH JEE LEONG, 30, discovered the joy of books at Radin Mas Primary School — "Beneath the Mount called Faber ..." — where he was also taught to love life by numerous teachers and friends. He is presently teaching Literature in a secondary school, where he is constantly surprised by the diverse interpretations a simple text can yield. Beautiful poetic forms captivates him, and he is convinced of our common need of "the best words in the best order."

FELIX LEE is a 21 year old Law student at NUS who fell in love with William Blake's brutality and Wilfred Owen's bitterness not too long ago. Far from claiming inspiration from them (and darkening their names), he attributes his writings to thought-patterns acquired in the hallucinatory state brought about by over-work and/or sleep-deprivation. Seek him out as Requiem on "poetry on galaxynet".

SHERRIE LEE does bits of reviewing and writing here and there but aspires to be a travel writer. She loves requiems, the cinematic experience, and Earl Grey on a cold morning. Whenever poetry reads like a dead fish, Wislawa Szymborska convinces her otherwise. Sherrie's philosophy for poetry is to transform simple incidents into profound truths. "I'm not writing the epic; I'm writing the intimate details you overlook."

A Singapore Cultural Medallionist (1985) and Southeast Asian WRITE Award winner (1987), LEE TZU PHENG is a pre-eminent figure in Singapore poetry. Her published works include 4 acclaimed volumes of poetry: *Prospect of a Drowning, Against the Next Wave, The Brink of An Amen* and *Lambada by Galilee* and numerous other publications. She is an Associate Professor at the Department of English Language and Literature, National University of Singapore.

DAVID LEO writes both poetry and short stories. Poetry writing began at a very early age, when the lyrical charm of Wordsworth, Coleridge and Keats captured him. In later years, he was much influenced by Yeats and Eliot. Feelings drive much of his writing. David enjoys travelling, swimming and indulges in day-dreaming whenever feasible. At the end of a hard day's work, he relaxes by doing crosswords, especially the cryptic kind.

LEONG LIEW GEOK is an Associate Professor in the Department of English Language & Literature, NUS. She has 2 poetry collections to her name and edited numerous anthologies and books, including Ee Tiang Hong's monograph, *Responsibility and Commitment: The Poetry of Edwin Thumboo* (1997), and *More than Half the Sky: Creative Writings by Thirty Singaporean Women* (1998). A plant addict and a rabid trial-and-error gardener, she is married and has three children.

SHIRLEY GEOK-LIN LIM is Chair Professor of English at the University of Hong Kong, and Professor of English and Women's Studies at the University of California, Santa Barbara. Her first collection of poems, *Crossing the Peninsula* (1980), received the Commonwealth Poetry Prize. She has published 4 volumes of poetry subsequently; the latest being *What the Fortune Teller Didn't Say* (1998). She was interviewed by Bill Moyers for a PBS special on American poetry in 1999. In her spare time, she sleeps and dreams of finding time for writing poetry.

Though fiction is his main preoccupation, JEFFREY LIM SUI YIN dabbles in poetry, having been published in *In Search of Words* (1991). 1999 saw the release of his first book of short stories, *Faith & Lies*. He is currently working on a new collection of short stories. "The Hanging People" was originally written in 1990 and was re-edited for this anthology.

JOHANN LOH RUNMING is a student. He reads Tristan Tzara and John Cage, drawing inspiration from their revilement of the conventional, the cliched and the bourgeois. The Dadaist revolution of art forms his basic beliefs — that art is not aesthetic wallpaper. Jazz is a source of depression, along with many other things in general.

SHANNON LOW is mobile. He did a degree in Philosophy and Economics, and then more Economics. He writes stuff, co-edits an e-mail magazine, organises and puts things together. Then he sits and watches. One day, when he goes back to the shop, he hopes to see long queues of people exchanging apathy for activism. That's why he writes.

LUO QINING is a full-time student at National Junior College. She gathers inspiration from observing Singaporeans, Singapore and fellow local poets cum friends; or she muses at the great poets like Keats and Auden. In her free time she juggles studies, chess, webpage and computer graphics design, writing and getting some sleep amidst the chaos (more affectionately called, "the prolonged blink between the time I get into bed and out of it").

GAYLE MAK graduated in Communication Studies, Nanyang Technological University in 1999. She now works in the civil service. Gayle stumbled upon creative writing in Primary Four and loves all things whimsical. Favourite books include Antoine Saint-Exupery's *The Little Prince*, Roald Dahl's *Charlie & the Chocolate Factory*, and A.A. Milne's *When We Were Very Young*.

NG YI-SHENG is a 19 year-old NSF. He writes occasional poetry, very occasional plays and prose, and lots of e-mail. He is inspired by shamefully little besides his literature texts, and, if truth be told, engages in the worship of Alfian Sa'at. He has been actively involved in the Creative Arts Programme and was mentored by Lee Tzu Pheng and Angeline Yap.

SERENE OW writes "Once upon a time, there was this girl who just wanted to write and write for the rest of her life. She was just a young kid then and young kids have a pretty wild imagination. Then, of course, things like school, parents and society seeped into the pages, and the little girl grew up. Now, all she does is write a bit every now and then. But she still dreams a lot ...."

ELAINE PANG most enjoys the wit and wordplay of the English language, and this has been a major focus in her poetry writing. Eighteen, formerly from Raffles Junior College, she is now waiting to enter a university to read English. In the interim, she maintains a website dedicated to poetry, and enjoys reading Jeanette Winterson and Neil Gaiman. She is also influenced by the poetry of Carol Ann Duffy and Sylvia Plath. Her website can be found at <http://www.stormloader.com/elly/>

PEK LISHI JANE turns 18 this year and is studying in the Humanities Programme at Hwa Chong Junior College. She has been writing for around two-thirds of this semi-fictional existence and finds it rather enjoyable (if head-ache-inducing at times). Other interests include debating, taekwondo, squash, Chinese chess, comic books and theatre. She tries her best to learn from writers such as Michael Ondaatje, Raymond Carver, Ernest Hemmingway and Julian Barnes. Website <http://www.geocities.com/SoHo/5456>

DESMOND SIM is an MA graduate from the National University of Singapore who is currently an Executive Director of a multi-disciplinary creative group. He has won various prestigious prizes for writing and drama including the Merit Award for The Singapore Literature Prize, prizes for short story and theatre writing, the JAL Summer Scholarship to Sophia University, the ACBC Gold Medal for Literature and the Fulbright Professional Program to NYU and University of Washington.

KIRPAL SINGH is a father of three. Having grown up in a small town in Malaysia and then a kampong here in Singapore, Kirpal is very sharply aware of "the urban" as space/mode/attitude to be negotiated. Kirpal has given readings of his work in numerous international festivals and his latest book *Catwalking* (1998) was very well received internationally. He is now with the Singapore Management University.

ALFRED SIEW is currently a writer with Singapore Press Holdings. He graduated from the School of Communication Studies at Nanyang Techonological University. Major influences include Philip Larkin, Albert Camus, Thomas Hardy, and of late, Jack Kerouac. Also, the "flavour" in local poetry strikes him mostly poignantly. When not working, he is either surfing the Web or playing some action game.

DAREN V. L. SHIAU is a prize-winning writer who has been compared to Vikram Seth. Over the years, his prose and verse have earned him various university and national literary honours. His novel *Heartland* won the Singapore Literature Prize Commendation Award in 1998. His poetry collection titled *Peninsular* has just been published. A freelance book reviewer with *The Straits Times*, his favourite poets are Wislawa Szymborska and Lee Tzu Pheng.

DOMINIC SOON spends most of his waking days at Hwa Chong Junior College, where he finds a certain amount of spiritual relief in playing squash, chess, and moving along corridors. He is inspired by the seemingly mundane, impressed by hidden intricacies, and flounders at finding a good balance between the two. Besides poetry, he is also an amateur web-designer with a little closet at <http://www.tinted.net/mrdom/>

ANGIE TAN is a student. Her hobbies include reading quirky fiction, talking to people on the Internet and chatting with friends while nursing mocha freezes.

For ELIZA TAN, sounds of thoughts, colours of images past and present, the taste of surroundings found unconsciously on her tongue, and feelings that come from touching inspires her. Writing (above all!), travelling, good poetry or novels taken in on still days, and museum-mornings make up many of her favourite moments. She enjoys reading, especially the works of the 20th century poets including those of Elizabeth Bishop, Sylvia Plath and Wallace Stevens.

KEITH TAN is a 25-year-old civil servant who's had a life-long affair with poetry. He loves music, and the outdoors — camping under the stars on a clear night, with good friends for company, and a good guitar, counts as one of his highest delights. T. S. Eliot, W. B. Yeats, Ben Okri, Anna Akhmatova, Osip Mandelstam, Seamus Heaney, Allen Tate and Wallace Stevens are just some of his many muses.

KLYTH TAN SOO-HONG lives in an HBD town around the harbour district of Keppel. At various times, he has been a sub-editor, journalist, writer and tutor. Klyth is a new (though not young) poet still trying to find his poetic meter. He enjoys reading Shakespeare, listens to a lot of pop music and watches MTV. He will soon be furthering his studies in Perth, Australia. He dedicates his poems in memory of his dearest father.

TAN BEE KEE (born 1978) is an NUS undergraduate majoring in English Language and Literature and Professor Thumboo's ex-student. She won the first prize for poetry in the 1998/1999 NUS Literary Society competition. Her poem, "The Eternal Triangle" will be published in *Singa* 30. She is interested in post-colonial theory and issues concerning local literature. Besides reading and writing, she plays the classical guitar, studies Japanese and enjoys travelling.

PAUL TAN has published 2 volumes of verse: *Curious Roads* (1994) which won a commendation award in the1993 Singapore Literature Prize and *Driving Into Rain* (1998) which won the merit award in the 1997 Singapore Literature Prize. Under the Ministry of Education's Creative Arts

Programme, he also mentors secondary and JC students and provides critique for their creative works. He was also a member of the 1999 Singapore's Writer's Festival organising committee.

TAN TIONG CHENG writes: "What interests me is the totalising effect of urban space, its transformations, its insistent self-reflexive framework between culture and capitalism. The thematics of spectatorship has reduced lives in the city to a phantasmagoria; spirits intoxicated with each other, copulating in a techno-superstructure of commodity fetishism. Everyone's lives are in the buildings we erect, the roads we pave, and our stories live in them. We exist as ghosts of the machine-future. I want to tell these stories."

SIMON SC TAY, LL.B Hons (NUS) LL.M (Harvard) teaches international and constitutional law at the Faculty of Law, NUS. He has written 5 books of poems, stories and essays: *Prism* (1980); *5* (1985); *Stand Alone* (1991); *Over Singapore* (1993); and *Alien Asian* (1997). He has twice been an International Writer at the University of Iowa and, in 1991, *Stand Alone* was short-listed for the Commonwealth Prize (Asia-Pacific). In 1996, he was named Young Artist of the Year. He currently serves as Nominated Member of Parliament.

TENG QIAN XI's (pre)occupations are writing, reading, art, design and playing the violin. Her writing is strongly influenced by modern American poetry, Anne Sexton and U. A. Fanthorpe. Favourite writers include Virginia Woolf and Jeanette Winterson. She is a passionate fan of the movie *Carrington*, jazz and Paul Klee. She is currently a student of Hwa Chong Junior College, and plans to live in London, Corfu or Madagascar.

TOH HSIEN MIN is a graduate student at Oxford University. He has published one verse collection, *Iambus*, and is working on a second.

Emeritus Professor EDWIN THUMBOO is a much-decorated poet laureate. He is a recipient of the NBDCS Book Award (1978, 1980), the SEA Write Award (1979), the Cultural Medallion (1980) and the ASEAN Cultural Award for Literature (1987). He has edited anthologies and published 4 poetry books including *Gods Can Die* and *A Third Map*. A former Dean of the NUS Arts Faculty, he now heads its Centre for the Arts.

A 29-year old Singapore Foreign Service Officer, UMEJ SINGH BHATIA studied English Literature at Cambridge University. He has worked as a journalist and television producer. Recent inspirations and influences include riding the modem, Playstation, the Bhagavad Gita, Greek tragedy, Satyajit Ray, Anton Chekov, Don Delillo and poets John Donne, T. S. Eliot, W. H. Auden, Keith Douglas and for dogged saintliness — his mother.

CYRIL WONG is a member of the Singapore Youth Choir as well as its subsidiary chamber group, The Ensemble Singers. He studied voice under mezzo-soprano Yang Jie. Currently a 2nd year student in NUS, majoring in Literature, he will be publishing his book of poems later this year.

WONG SHIN MING was born in 1981 in a KL suburb. He underwent primary and secondary education in Singapore, spent two years in an English boarding school, and is now in Stanford, eyeing a Philosophy major. He counts everything he has come into contact with as an influence, and understands but rejects the attribution of ideas to specific people, since ideas belong to us all.

ANGELINE YAP, wife, lawyer, writer and working mother of three, thirstily soaks up children's literature to relax. Angeline started writing during her convent schooldays and has contributed poems to various anthologies since the 1970s. One of the more recent is the popular *More Than Half The Sky* (1998). Literary influences include Shakespeare, Wilfred Owen, Robert Frost, Madeleine L'Engle, CS Lewis, Luci Shaw. Currently reading Jane Kenyon and Donald Hall.

Poet, Painter and Teacher, ARTHUR YAP has published several volumes of poetry, the latest being *the space of city trees* by Skoob Books, London. Arthur has held numerous solo exhibitions at the National Library and at Alpha Gallery between 1969–1977. He was awarded the Southeast Asian WRITE Award and the Singapore Cultural Medallion in 1983, and in 1998, he received the Mont Blanc-CFA Award. He is curently enjoying retirement.

JOSHUA YAP (born 1982) is a vaguely harassed student who thinks Cummings and Yeats should have met Li Bai and written a martial arts novel in experimental blank verse. Enjoys soft music, loud poems, and was mentored by Lee Tzu Pheng and Heng Siok Tian respectively under the auspices of the Creative Arts Programme.

DENNIS YEO is a student at Anglo-Chinese School (Independent). In 1998, he underwent mentorship with Ho Poh Fun in the Creative Arts Programme. Reading and writing both interest him, although circumstances have been hindering his devoting time to them recently. He debates, uses computers quite often and wishes he had more time to do other things, like getting started on his near-interminable reading list and roaming the city.

ROBERT YEO is an Associate Professor in the National Institute of Education, NTU. His latest book *Leaving Home, Mother* (1999) contains poems he had written in the last 3 decades. He has also written plays and in 1999, a third staging of his short play "Second Chance" took place. Robert has also published a novel called *The Adventures of Holden Heng*. In 2000, he hopes to see his trilogy of plays published.

YEOW KAI CHAI won 1st prize in poetry for 2 consecutive years at NUS. He admires artists who shun intellectual solipsism and continuously probe self-representations, from radical abstract poet John Yau to humane, visionary songsmiths Caetano Veloso, Arto Lindsay and Sinead O'Connor. He hopes to get his first collection "The Dumb Creatures", which was shortlisted for the 1995 Singapore Literature Prize, published soon.

YIP SAU LENG is a freelance assistant producer/director/scriptwriter. She devours whatever or whoever captures her curiosity — pop culture, renaissance art, *The Little Prince*, Dorothy Parker, world history, *On The Road*, Gabriel Garcia Marquez, feminism, Roald Dahl, Oscar Wilde, *The English Patient*, astronomy, W. H. Auden are just a few. Inspiration comes from life itself and she believes that every book she's read has influenced her in one way or another.

CALEB YONG is currently attending secondary school. While Romantic literature leaves him largely disinterested, he thanks Baudelaire, Rimbaud and Appollinaire for giving the world literary modernity. He finds the Imagists unforgettable, and is still discovering Pablo Neruda and Ted Hughes. The black-and-white of Sally Mann and Robert Doisneau are more beautiful than any Renaissance oil-on-canvas. And his discman may begin to tire of Thomas Adès.

YONG SHU HOONG studied computer science and business in National University of Singapore and Texas A&M University at College Station respectively. He enjoys different forms of writing — from music reviews to poetry. His first book of poems, *Isaac*, was published in 1997. Currently working for an Internet company, he also enjoys travelling, watching movies, and surfing the net.

ZARINA MUHAMMAD is a 2nd year student in the arts faculty at Catholic Junior College. She started writing poetry 2 years ago. Aside from poetry, her interests also lie in playwriting and drama. Her work is influenced by music, especially that of artiste Tori Amos, sculptures, modern life, people and as of late, surrealist paintings and works by poets Margaret Atwood and Sylvia Plath.

INDEX

Poem titles are in italics and name of poets are in alphabetical order according to their family names.

D

E

F

G

H

I

J

K

L

M

N

O